Konditor & Cook

Konditor & Cook

Deservedly Legendary Baking ...

... now at Your fingertips,

enjoy!

Gerw Jenne

Gerhard Jenne

EBURY
PRESS

Contents

Foreword

Well, the lid is truly off what was once one of my most loved little secrets, Konditor & Cook, and I couldn't be happier for Gerhard and his team of expert bakers. Their marvellous cakes and pastries deserve to be known the world over because they make it a happier and hungrier place.

Baking might be all the rage at the moment but this marvellous success story began many, many years ago on a charming little street in the Waterloo Conservation area, in a shop that smells deliciously of coffee, chocolate and caramel. I remember my first visit: it was like entering a fairyland imagined by Hans Christian Andersen, filled with the most wondrous cakes and pastries that not only looked magical but tasted divine too. I was hooked from the start and although they may have spread their wings a little further, Konditor & Cook has lost none of its charm.

They also bake cakes to order and my family have commissioned spectacular cakes for two of my birthdays that stole the show and were a talking point for weeks afterwards. The last one was a huge tower overflowing with smaller cakes that represented all my favourite things, such as lobsters, cigars, wines, roses, cars and Monsieur Bibendum, the Michelin man. Gerhard's imagination combined brilliantly with his exceptional baking skills takes Konditor & Cook's products to another level entirely.

To my mind, the secret of Konditor & Cook's success is that they are creative and committed to using the highest-quality ingredients in their products, using only free-range eggs and the best flours available. Their dried fruits are first rate and they take great care baking in controllable quantities, which makes them perfectly placed to write a book about baking and sprinkle their magic over kitchens across the land.

Whether it is creating a wonderful show-stopper or making something simple with the kids, baking really is one of life's great pleasures. So put on your apron, delve into the secrets and recipes of Konditor & Cook and enjoy the delights of baking their magical cakes in your own kitchen.

Sir Terence Conran

Introduction

This book is a reflection of two decades of baking, from delicious everyday recipes to decadent cake creations fit for a queen. In it, I would like to share with you some of the most popular recipes from Konditor & Cook's early years, as well as those that have stood the test of time and become legendary – recipes such as our Raspberry Fudge Tart, Boston Brownies, Kipferl Cookies, Curly Whirly Cake and, of course, the Magic Cakes that we used to create a giant portrait of the Queen, which went on display at Battersea Park for the Diamond Jubilee celebration. I hope you will be able to bring them to life in your own kitchen and make them *your* recipes, too.

I have often said that at Konditor & Cook every cake has a story behind it – whether it's the inspiration for a magnificent tiered cake, how a particular recipe came about, or what it is in a recipe that has made it so irresistible over time.

I hope that, in these pages, I have captured some of the Konditor & Cook magic that made Sir Terence Conran include his favourite London cake shop in a list of the top 100 retail stores in the world.

Ever since I trained as a baker and pastry chef in Germany, I dreamed of opening my own *Konditorei*. A *Konditorei* can be defined as a cake shop; most often it is a combination of shop and café. The shop offers a wide range of cakes and confections with seasonal variations, while in the café you can enjoy the entire spread of baking as well as a menu of small savoury dishes.

In order to fulfil my dream, I needed to save some money and gain more experience. This eventually brought me to London, where, after a stint at the now defunct Swiss Centre in Leicester Square, I ended up working for inspirational food entrepreneur Justin de Blank in Knightsbridge. It was there that I honed my skills in essential British baking and was at the forefront of the British food revolution of the 1980s. As well as introducing some of my own recipes, I developed an interest in one-off cake creations for celebrity customers, including Tina Turner, Ringo Starr and The Rolling Stones.

One of the best things about Justin de Blank was that the cooks were expected to interact with the customers. It made the preparation of

food all the more enjoyable, as we would often get immediate feedback. I really enjoyed the exchanges with the customers and was bursting to set up on my own. I just needed a space where I could put my vision into place.

After a combination of failed attempts and nerves, it so happened that in the summer of 1993 my attention was drawn to a small bakery in Waterloo. The Queen of Hearts Bakery on Cornwall Road was about to close down and needed a new owner. At the time, the area was still suffering from the economic plight caused by the closure of the Greater London Council, and was about to be thrown into further turmoil thanks to the excavation works associated with the imminent extension of the Jubilee line.

Despite all this, I saw a perfect little set up: a beautiful small shop front at the end of a terrace of late-Georgian artisan cottages with a production kitchen right behind. Since it was near the station, it enjoyed great footfall to the offices along the river, and, as it turned out much later, the South Bank was to be transformed further with the development of the London Eye and Tate Modern.

All the shop needed was a lick of paint, a new name and, more importantly, a complete set of new recipes and a revised approach to quality, for the previous incumbent had the reputation of producing some rather fusty-looking pies and tarts. When it came to naming the shop, I drew inspiration from my training as a pastry chef, or *Konditor*, in Germany and from my acquisition of skills in savoury cooking (Cook) at Justin de Blank in London.

In those days people weren't used to going into cake shops. The idea was to provide a lure with the provision of a range of 'daily bread' savouries but then to tempt customers, once inside, with plates full of freshly baked pastries, mouth-watering mountains of brownies and enticing layered sponge cakes.

At the time, Waterloo was notorious for its Cardboard City housing the homeless in

the Bullring. With Konditor & Cook a mere stone's throw away, I wanted to signal that this could be an area of 'hope'. Since then, the area has changed hugely and the Bullring is now home to the BFI's IMAX cinema.

The shop was painted a rich, plummy purple that contrasted perfectly with the white china used for our displays and complemented the appetising colours of the fresh baking. When a large number of different baked goods are on display in a shop, it looks better if there is a unifying theme running through the choice of china. At home you can be more liberal, and I hope the beautiful photos in this book will inspire you to be adventurous with the presentation of your baking. The final setting of the food is a vital ingredient in how it is perceived and tasted.

Our commitment to quality, including the use of organic eggs and natural butter in all our baking, was printed on our first paper bags. Eggs are one of the most important ingredients when it comes to baking. Freshness is important but I have always been of the opinion that eggs laid by happy hens are superior in their make up and flavour.

I also prefer butter to margarine, but take a more liberal view on salted versus unsalted. Lightly salted butter enhances the flavour of cakes and the salt content is low in comparison to the basket of other ingredients in most recipes. Sometimes, of course, it is important to use unsalted butter and this will always be stated in the recipes.

Generally when it comes to the quality of ingredients there's no point in skimping. Chocolate, nuts, sugar, fruit – it is well worth seeking out the ones with the best flavour. In some ways you get out only what you put in.

It is through the ingredients we use and our desire to show the honesty of our products that the simple Konditor & Cook style evolved. I'm not into overtly sophisticated-looking concoctions that taste of nothing. My baking has to have depth of flavour.

When I trained in Germany, the only decorating materials considered acceptable were marzipan, chocolate and red jam, and most designs were somewhat stuck in the past. I've always thought of myself as a cake decorator for the rock 'n' roll generation. This means that, besides embracing a bit of food colouring, I have drawn on influences by artists such as Mackintosh, Klimt, Matisse, Lichtenstein and Yayoi Kusama, to name but a few. It's good to have your finger on the contemporary pulse in decorating.

Konditor & Cook's enthusiasm for new recipes and innovative formats, as well as our love of using them for seasonal ideas, has given us a great following among the cake cognoscenti and led to stores in Borough Market and Holborn, as well as our largest store and bakery in London landmark the Gherkin, described as 'the hottest bakery in the City of London since 1666'.

In the twenty years since Konditor & Cook opened, there have been significant changes in Britain's attitude to food. There are now many more artisanal producers and thriving farmers' markets selling wonderful ingredients, and there has been a revival of interest in home baking.

There's never been a better time to pick up a bowl and whisk and try some recipes at home. British supermarket aisles are brimming with a wide variety of baking ingredients, making the job of shopping for them so much easier. This all goes hand in hand with a thirst for new recipes. German baking has been overlooked to a large extent. Here's your chance to be ahead of the pack and delight in some of the recipes from my home country that have influenced the Konditor & Cook repertoire. Is there anything better than a slice of freshly baked Nusszopf? Mind you, I could say that about all the recipes, since I'm a very keen cake-eater indeed.

When Nigella Lawson wrote about Konditor & Cook in *Vogue* magazine, she summed it up perfectly: 'the sort of cakes you'd make yourself if only you had the time, energy or inclination to do so'. With this collection of recipes, I'm giving you the opportunity to bake the Konditor & Cook way. And most of them won't require a lot of time or energy, just enthusiasm and a keen appetite.

These recipes are here for you to have fun with, and to spark your own imagination. Once you've enjoyed success with the simpler recipes, you may want to embark on the more ambitious decorative projects in the Fun and Festivities chapter.

The way I approach cake decoration is to do it without relying too much on specialist equipment. This gives you the chance to create your own versions of the decorative cakes at home, based on the advice given in this book. They don't rely on perfection for their appeal either. A bit of wit and a personal touch are much better crowd pleasers than that perfectly placed rosette.

If something doesn't quite go to plan, don't lose faith. Often a cake disaster gives birth to something fresh and new. Quite a few of Konditor & Cook's recipes have come about this way. As long as it tastes delicious, you have succeeded.

Gerhard Jenne
www.konditorandcook.com

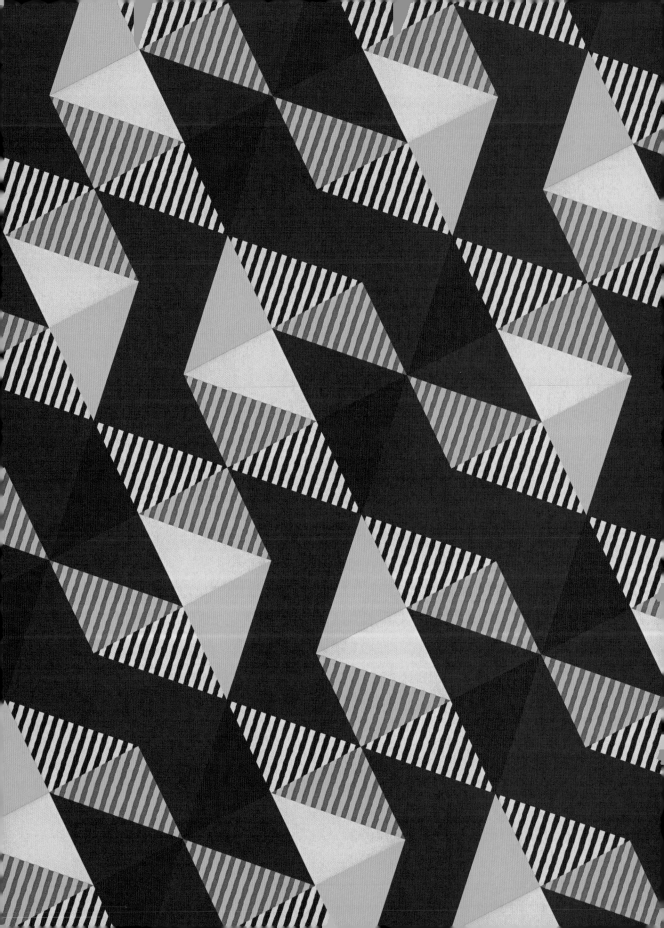

Cakes

Curly Whirly Cake

When Konditor & Cook opened in 1993, the dark chocolate cake was our most popular. Chocolate throughout, it was filled with a rich ganache. One of its biggest fans was a Mrs Simon of Sloane Square, who always bought it for family birthdays, until one Thanksgiving when she requested a vanilla filling instead of the customary ganache. And that's when the Curly Whirly Cake was born – a dark chocolate sponge laden with creamy vanilla frosting.

At the time, we also went through a Klimt-inspired wedding-cake period. Gold-leaf squares and decorative swirls were all the rage, and so it was that an everyday cake ended up with some pretty chocolate curly-whirly decorations.

The Curly Whirly has topped the number-one spot ever since, and I hope this recipe will make it an equally staple part of your baking.

Makes a 17cm cake

For the dark
chocolate sponge:

250ml milk

275g light soft brown sugar

**100g dark chocolate
(54 per cent cocoa
solids), chopped**

175g plain flour

1 tsp baking powder

30g cocoa powder

100g salted butter, softened

**2 medium eggs,
lightly beaten**

To decorate:

**1 quantity of Cream Cheese
Frosting, flavoured with
vanilla (see page 211)**

**chocolate flakes
or a little melted
chocolate (optional)**

Heat the oven to 190°C/Gas Mark 5. Line two 17cm sandwich tins with foil or baking parchment.

Heat half the milk and half the soft brown sugar together in a saucepan until the sugar has dissolved, then add the chocolate and stir over a low heat until melted. Remove from the heat and leave to cool slightly.

Sift the flour, baking powder and cocoa powder together and set aside. Put the butter in a large bowl, add the remaining sugar and beat together until light and fluffy, using an electric mixer. Gradually add the beaten eggs, alternating each addition with a tablespoon of the flour mixture to prevent it splitting.

Fold in the rest of the flour, followed by the remaining milk, then add the still-warm chocolate milk. Mix until smooth; it will have a very runny consistency.

Divide the mixture between the 2 lined tins and bake for 20–25 minutes, until risen and firm to the touch. Remove from the oven and leave to cool in the tins.

Turn the cakes out of their tins and sandwich them together with about a quarter of the frosting. Spread a thin layer of frosting over the top and sides to bind any crumbs and then leave to set in the fridge for an hour.

Coat with the remaining frosting, smoothing it with a palette knife. Sprinkle with chocolate flakes or put the melted chocolate in a parchment piping bag (see page 216) and pipe patterns on the cake.

Victoria Sponge Cake

Every baker in the land must have a recipe for this most British of cakes. Or if not a recipe, then certainly an opinion or a memory: 'My grandmother's Victoria sponge was the best.' Discovering a great recipe for a Victoria sponge is almost on a par with finding the path to spiritual enlightenment.

Perhaps Grandmother's recipe was better because in the past they could afford to take their time over beating the ingredients. On the other hand, our modern equipment is much more efficient. I haven't had much luck with recipes that involve chucking everything in a bowl and simply letting it whizz round for 10 minutes. I err on the traditional side, looking for a light sponge with a fine porosity of crumb. Unusually, though, this recipe includes a little crème fraîche. It adds more fat, which results in a finer texture and reduces the risk of the mixture curdling, while the extra egg yolk gives the batter more stability and keeps the sponge moist. Usually, the higher the egg white content, the drier the cake.

I have suggested filling and finishing the cake the way we do it at Konditor & Cook, but you can vary this as you like. Strawberry jam and whipped double cream make fine companions, and my friend Ben swears by clotted cream and fresh raspberries – a less sweet option. The jammy heart we pipe on the sponge is an expression of the enduring love we hold for this cake.

Hopefully this recipe will take you a step further on your path to baking enlightenment.

Makes a 20cm cake

4 medium eggs

1 egg yolk

225g self-raising flour

200g salted butter, softened

¼ tsp vanilla extract

225g caster sugar

75ml crème fraîche

To finish:

125g raspberry jam,
    plus 2 tbsp for piping
    the heart

½ quantity of Cream
    Cheese Frosting,
    flavoured with vanilla
    (see page 211)

1 tbsp icing sugar

Heat the oven to 165°C/Gas Mark 3. At Konditor & Cook we make this cake in two 20cm sandwich tins with gently sloping sides and line them with foil. This means the sponge shows off its golden colour nicely and the sloping sides give the filled cake a slightly concave look, as if it has a waist. I have found that buttering and flour dusting the tin makes the cake look dry.

Break the eggs and egg yolk into a measuring jug (the exact quantity of egg is crucial; you need 225ml) and beat briefly with a fork or a few turns of an electric hand mixer. Sift the self-raising flour into a bowl and set aside.

Put the butter, vanilla extract and sugar in a bowl and beat with an electric mixer on medium speed for 4 minutes, until light and fluffy. Add the crème fraîche and beat for a minute longer; this will add more volume and help to dissolve the sugar crystals.

Continued...

Reduce the speed of the mixer and add the beaten eggs and the flour in 6–8 alternate additions, retaining a smooth emulsion and taking care to prevent the mixture splitting. If you add the equivalent of just under 1 egg, beat it in well, then reduce the speed more and add 2 tablespoons of flour, making sure the ingredients are thoroughly mixed in before the next addition, it should be fine. When all the egg has been added, gently fold in the remaining flour with a large spatula. The mixture should look white and be soft enough to fall nicely off the spatula.

Divide the mixture equally between the lined tins and bake for 25 minutes, then check if the cakes are done by inserting a skewer or a small knife into the centre – if it comes out clean, the cakes are ready. Alternatively, press gently on the centre of the sponge; if it springs back, it is done. If the cakes need more time, reduce the heat a little and bake for 2–3 minutes longer. Remove from the oven, leave to cool in the tins for 10 minutes, then turn out on to a wire rack to cool completely.

Carefully peel off the foil and place one cake upside down on a plate or cake board. Spread the jam over the top. Turn the second cake upside down on to a separate board and spread with the frosting. Flip the frosted layer on to the jam layer, make sure it is centred and then press gently into place with the flat of your hand. For a simple finish, dust with icing sugar.

For the heart finish, cut a heart template out of baking parchment, place it on top of the cake and dust with icing sugar. Lift off the paper, being careful not to spill any of the icing sugar. Pass the 2 tablespoons of raspberry jam through a fine sieve to remove the seeds. Make a parchment piping bag (see page 216), fill it with the jam, then snip a 2–3mm opening. Pipe swirls on to the sponge to fill the heart, then finish it with a line of small dots, 1cm apart, around the edge. Ideally half of each dot will be on the sugar-dusted part of the cake, the other half on the undusted part, to give the heart a lacy look.

Coffee and Walnut Cake

This cake has always been in our repertoire but I very nearly didn't include it in this book, as it seems so old-fashioned – a far cry from a cronut. Yet it's the baking equivalent of the nautilus: it has been around for years but still has amazing appeal. To avoid any outcry, I decided I had better include it.

The reason for its popularity is probably that walnuts and coffee are a fantastic flavour combination. And, as so often in baking, a bit of nostalgia might also be behind its enduring success. Here is the recipe as we present it in the shops. It's pretty traditional and has not yet been subjected to remastering into the 'flat white' equivalent of coffee cakes. Perhaps this is going to be your bake-off challenge.

Makes a 21cm cake

175g self-raising flour

150g salted butter, softened

150g caster sugar

1½ tbsp ground coffee

50g walnuts, ground

1 tsp instant coffee,
    dissolved in just enough
    hot water to make a paste

3 medium eggs, beaten

For the coffee syrup:

1 tbsp honey

50g caster sugar

1 tbsp instant coffee

For the frosting:

½ quantity of Cream
    Cheese Frosting
    (see page 211)

1 tbsp instant coffee,
    mixed to a paste with
    a little hot water

For the caramelised
walnuts (optional):

2 tbsp caster sugar

50g whole or halved walnuts

Heat the oven to 180°C/Gas Mark 4. To give this cake a slightly rustic look, cut a 36cm square of baking parchment, run it under the tap to wet it, then scrunch it into a ball. Wring out the excess water, open the paper up again and mould it into a 21cm round cake tin. Where it creases, you will later have the lines that give the cake an authentic look. If you prefer straight sides, simply butter the tin and line the base with baking parchment.

Sift the flour and set aside. Using an electric mixer, beat the butter, caster sugar and ground coffee together until pale and fluffy. Mix in the ground walnuts and the coffee paste.

Beat in about a quarter of the eggs, then reduce the speed and add a tablespoon of the flour. Repeat the process until all the egg is mixed in, then gently fold in the remainder of the flour.

Transfer the mixture to the prepared tin and level the top. Bake for about 30 minutes, until a skewer inserted in the centre comes out clean. Remove from the oven and leave to cool for 30 minutes.

While the cake is in the oven, prepare the coffee syrup: put the honey and sugar in a small saucepan, add 75ml water and bring to the boil, stirring to dissolve the sugar. Remove from the heat, add the instant coffee and stir until dissolved.

Continued...

If you are including the caramelised walnuts, put the sugar in a small, heavy-based pan, add 3 tablespoons of water and bring to the boil, stirring to dissolve the sugar. Simmer until it starts to thicken, then add the walnuts. Cook, stirring, until all the water has evaporated and the walnuts are caramelised, then remove them from the pan and spread them out on a piece of baking parchment. It doesn't matter if the nuts stick together a little bit but they shouldn't all clump together.

Turn the cake out of the tin, remove the baking parchment and put the cake on a cake board or flat plate. Prick the surface a few times with a fork, more so around the edges than the middle. Using a pastry brush, brush the coffee syrup on the top, starting around the edge and moving into the middle. You can also brush the sides a little bit. Do this while the cake and syrup are still a little warm, as the syrup will be absorbed more easily. Leave to soak and set in the fridge for 1 hour.

Mix the frosting with the instant coffee paste. Using a spoon or palette knife, spread the frosting over the top of the cake. Serve as is or decorate with a border of caramelised walnuts.

Mela Cannella

Those familiar with Italian will have spotted that this cake features apples and cinnamon. It also contains blackberries, making it a great autumnal cake.

The recipe was inspired by some Italian customers who were attending a language course near our Waterloo shop. One day we got talking and they mentioned that they missed a cake featuring cinnamon. Next thing, this very moist upside-down cake was tempting them and others into the shop on a daily basis. A show-stopping rustic centrepiece, it is at its most delicious served still slightly warm, with cream.

Makes a 25cm cake

700g cooking apples
   (about 600g prepared
   weight)

275g caster sugar

100g raisins

300g self-raising flour

½ tsp baking powder

125g salted butter,
   softened

1½ tsp ground cinnamon

¼ tsp vanilla extract

3 medium eggs,
   lightly beaten

50ml milk

150g fresh or frozen
   blackberries

75g apricot jam,
   for glazing (optional)

Heat the oven to 180°C/Gas Mark 4. Line a 25cm round cake tin with foil or baking parchment.

Peel the apples, core them and cut into thin segments. Mix 200g of the apples with 2 tablespoons of the caster sugar and set aside.

Put the remaining apples in a saucepan, add 4 tablespoons of water and cook until they are beginning to soften. Remove from the heat, stir in the raisins and leave to cool.

Sift the flour and baking powder into a bowl and set aside. Using an electric mixer, beat the softened butter with the remaining sugar, plus the cinnamon and vanilla, for about 3 minutes, until really light and fluffy.

Beat in about a quarter of the beaten eggs, then reduce the speed and add a tablespoon of the flour. Repeat until all the egg is mixed in, then mix in another tablespoon of flour. Add the milk and mix that in too. Gently fold in the remainder of the flour. Finally fold in the apple and raisin mixture.

Sprinkle the blackberries and the reserved apples over the base of the lined tin, then top with the cake mixture. Bake for 10 minutes, then reduce the oven temperature to 165°C/Gas Mark 3 and bake for a further 40 minutes, until the cake is springy to the touch and a knife inserted in the centre comes out clean.

Leave to cool in the tin for about 30 minutes, then turn out upside down and carefully peel off the foil or baking parchment.

If you want to glaze the cake, heat the jam in a small pan until hot and runny. If it has bits of fruit in it, you will need to strain it through a fine sieve into a small bowl. Brush it all over the still slightly warm cake.

Stem Ginger Cake

We recently stopped baking this cake to make room for something new in the shops. There was a lot of protest from our regulars, so here's the opportunity for you to bake your own. Or you could wait for it to come back on the cake list, which is usually around Christmas time.

Copious amounts of candied stem ginger give this cake its spicy, gingery, sweet taste. It's very soft and moist and, sealed under its simple lemon icing, it keeps really well – that's if you can resist it. Or do as some restaurants did when we used to supply them with this cake: omit the icing and lightly warm the cake in a microwave or oven before serving, then pass it off as a 'steamed ginger pudding'.

Makes a 26cm cake

250g self-raising flour

325g salted butter, softened

250g caster sugar

50g black treacle

1 tbsp ground ginger

50g ground almonds

5 medium eggs,
   lightly beaten

125ml milk

100g stem ginger in syrup,
   chopped

For the lemon icing:

200g icing sugar

juice and grated zest
   of 1 unwaxed lemon

To decorate (optional):

2 tbsp flaked almonds,
   light toasted

2 bulbs of stem ginger,
   finely sliced

candied lemon zest
   (made following
   the recipe for
   Candied Orange Zest
   on page 161)

Heat the oven to 165°C/Gas Mark 3. Line the base of a 26cm springform cake tin with baking parchment.

Sift the flour into a bowl and set aside. Using an electric mixer, beat the butter with the sugar, treacle and ground ginger for about 5 minutes, until the mixture is light and fluffy. Then mix in the ground almonds.

Beat in about a fifth of the beaten eggs, then reduce the speed and add a tablespoon of the flour. Repeat until all the egg is mixed in, then mix in another tablespoon of flour. Add the milk and mix that in too. Gently fold in the remainder of the flour. Add the chopped stem ginger and fold in until evenly distributed.

Turn the mixture into the prepared tin, level the top and bake for 15 minutes. Reduce the oven temperature to 150°C/Gas Mark 2 and bake for a further 45 minutes, until a skewer inserted in the centre comes out clean. Remove from the oven and leave to cool.

To make the icing, sift the icing sugar into a bowl, add the lemon zest, then gradually stir in enough lemon juice to make a thickish paste.

Turn the cake upside down and peel off the baking parchment. Turn it the right way up again and spread the lemon icing on it with a palette knife or the back of a spoon. Decorate with flaked almonds, thin slices of ginger and candied lemon zest, if liked.

Henrietta's Tipsy Cake

It was my friend Henrietta Ott who inspired me to come to London in the early 1980s. She had lived in London herself and knew it was a city of great contrasts and tradition but also one of freedom and creativity. We used to bake this elegant, fine-textured chocolate cake when living together in Munich. At Christmas it gets another outing in the form of Mulled Wine Cupcakes (see page 188) topped with a spiced mascarpone frosting.

Makes a 25cm cake

250g self-raising flour

½ tsp ground cinnamon

2 tsp cocoa powder

200g salted butter, softened

175g caster sugar

¼ tsp vanilla extract

4 medium eggs, lightly beaten

125ml red wine

100g dark chocolate (54 per cent cocoa solids), melted

1 quantity of Chocolate Icing (see page 213)

To decorate (optional):

50g caster sugar

50ml red wine

100g raisins, preferably crimson raisins

Heat the oven to 180°C/Gas Mark 4. Grease and lightly flour a 25cm round cake tin – a bundt tin or other ornate cake tin works well here.

Sift the flour, cinnamon and cocoa powder together and set aside. Using an electric mixer, beat the butter, caster sugar and vanilla extract together until light and fluffy.

Add the beaten eggs a little at a time to the mixture, alternating each addition with a tablespoon of the flavoured flour. Then add the red wine in the same fashion to prevent the mixture splitting. Gently fold in the remaining flour, followed by the melted chocolate.

Transfer the mixture to the prepared cake tin and bake for 60–70 minutes, until a skewer inserted in the centre comes out clean. Remove from the oven and leave to cool in the tin for 30 minutes, then turn out on to a wire rack to cool completely.

If you want to decorate the cake with wine-soaked raisins, put the sugar and red wine in a pan and bring to the boil, stirring to dissolve the sugar. Add the raisins and leave to cool.

Apply the chocolate icing to the top and sides of the cake using a pastry brush. Drain the raisins and sprinkle them over the cake.

Almond St Clement Cake

One of the questions I have been asked most often over the years is which is my favourite cake. This gluten-free recipe is definitely in the top ten. It is very moist, refreshingly indulgent and can be transformed into a lovely pudding.

Enjoy its juicy fruitiness plain, or add some Greek yoghurt and fresh fruit or a quick summer berry compote.

Makes a 24cm cake

3 large unwaxed oranges

1 unwaxed lemon

5 medium eggs

250g ground almonds

1 tsp baking powder

325g caster sugar

60g flaked almonds

Heat the oven to 165°C/Gas Mark 3. Line the base of a 24cm springform cake tin with baking parchment. There is no need to grease the side of the tin, as the cake will shrink away from it during baking.

Remove the zest from the oranges and lemon and set aside. Juice the lemon and one of the oranges and set the juice aside, too. Place the remaining 2 oranges in a saucepan, cover with water and bring to the boil. Simmer for 1 hour, then remove the oranges from the water and leave to cool.

Peel the cooked oranges and reduce the flesh to a pulp, either in a food processor or using a stick blender. Add the eggs and the reserved zest and blitz until smooth.

Mix the ground almonds, baking powder and 250g of the sugar together in a bowl, add the orange and egg mixture and mix with a wooden spoon until smooth.

Pour the mixture into the lined tin and sprinkle the flaked almonds around the edge. Bake for about 30 minutes, until risen and golden brown. Remove from the oven and leave to cool a little.

Place the remaining sugar and the reserved lemon and orange juice in a small saucepan and bring to the boil, stirring to dissolve the sugar. Simmer over a medium heat for about 5 minutes to make a syrup.

Turn the cake out of the tin while it is still warm and pour or brush the hot syrup over it. Leave to cool completely.

Sunken Pear and Black Gingerbread Cake

Once the clocks go back and the nights draw in, we change our range of cakes at Konditor & Cook, with light summer bakes making way for autumnal and then Christmas recipes.

The sponge part of this recipe can be baked as a loaf cake or cupcakes (see page 169). Combining it with caramelised pears, however, adds another dimension. Although the cake can be enjoyed with a cup of tea, the pears give it dessert status. Served warm, with a little pouring cream on the side, it is scrumptious and one of my favourites.

Makes a 25cm cake

250g plain flour

1 tbsp ground cinnamon

1 tbsp ground ginger

2 tsp bicarbonate of soda

175g light soft brown sugar

200ml milk

175g salted butter, softened

175g black treacle

2 medium eggs, lightly beaten

For the pears:

75g salted butter

150g light soft brown sugar

4 large or 6 small pears, such as Conference, peeled, quartered and cored

Heat the oven to 150°C/Gas Mark 2. Line a 25cm cake tin with foil. If you only have narrow foil, criss-cross 2 sheets to make sure the sides are covered and that there is a lip of at least 1cm all round to contain any juices.

First cook the pears. Put the butter and soft brown sugar in a pan and heat gently until dissolved. Raise the heat and simmer for about 5 minutes, until it becomes a light caramel; it will look like an even, bubbling cauldron when it is ready. Pour the caramel into the foil-lined cake tin, then fan the pears out on top like a sunflower, with the rounded part of the pear facing downwards. Set aside.

To make the cake, sift the flour with the spices and bicarbonate of soda and set aside. Slowly heat the brown sugar and milk in a pan (you can use the one you used for the caramel). By the time you are ready to use the mixture, it should just be starting to simmer.

Using an electric mixer, beat the butter and treacle together until they become paler. Gradually beat in the eggs, then, using the mixer on slow speed, add the sifted flour and mix until it is all combined. Slowly and carefully add the hot milk mix and blend to a runny consistency.

Pour the mixture over the pears in the tin and bake for about an hour, until a skewer inserted in the centre comes out clean.

Remove from the oven and leave to cool in the tin for an hour. Then turn the cake out upside down on to a cake board or flat plate and remove the foil. Be careful not to tear the pears away with the foil. You can avoid this by making a small cut in the foil in the centre of the cake, then gently peel away strips of foil from the centre, moving outwards.

Nusszopf (Twisted Hazelnut Loaf)

On holiday, I always make a point of checking out the local bakeries to see if there are any regional specialities. In France, I fell in love with the crème-mousseline-filled tarte tropézienne while on holiday near St Tropez, and a fig-filled brioche had me humming when in Uzès. The Nusszopf is the archetypal bake of southern Germany. It is light enough to have with milky coffee in the morning or with a cup of tea for elevenses, or perhaps a small helping for the traditional *Kaffeeklatsch* at 4 p.m. (followed by something more indulgent!). It's also rather good with a glass of medium-dry white wine in the evening. In fact, the Nusszopf tends to be present from the cradle to the grave! For extra naughtiness, I have been known to spread my slice with unsalted butter.

One note of caution: while the cake is simple to make, this is not a recipe you can knock up in 30 minutes. It takes 3–4 hours, but for most of that time you can be relaxing or doing something else while the yeast does all the work.

Makes a 30–40cm loaf

1 quantity of Bun Dough
  (see page 209)

80g icing sugar

40g skinned hazelnuts,
  lightly crushed
  (optional)

For the hazelnut filling:

125g ground hazelnuts

125g caster sugar

125g sweet crumbs
  (use sponge cake, scones
  or a mix of bread crumbs
  and digestive biscuits,
  whizzed in a blender)

1 medium egg

1 tsp ground cinnamon

½ tsp ground mixed spice

¼ tsp vanilla extract

a few tablespoons of milk

First prepare the hazelnut filling. Some ground hazelnuts are available to buy pre-toasted. Alternatively, heat the oven to 180°C/ Gas Mark 4, spread the ground nuts out on a baking tray lined with baking parchment and toast in the oven for 5–7 minutes, until light brown. Remove from the oven and leave to cool.

Put all the ingredients for the filling in a bowl and mix with a spatula, adding enough milk to give a spreadable consistency. You can add more or different spices if you want to be creative.

When the bun dough has risen to twice its size, roll it out on a lightly floured surface into a rough 40cm square. It's best to roll diagonally as well as from top to bottom, lifting the dough up regularly and turning it 180 degrees. Dust with a little more flour as necessary.

Spread the nut filling evenly over the dough, leaving about 3cm clear at the end nearest you. Pick up the end of the dough furthest away from you and roll it towards you into a log. Rest it on its seam.

Continued...

Using a small, sharp serrated knife, cut the dough lengthways down the middle. With the pieces lying next to each other, showing their stripy innards, pick up the end of the strands and start twisting from the middle, twisting the strands towards you. Repeat the twist with the other two ends.

Grease a baking sheet or line it with baking parchment and lay the twist on it. It should be 30–40cm long. Cover loosely with a sheet of cling film to prevent a skin forming and leave to prove for at least 45 minutes, until it has nearly doubled in size.

Heat the oven to 180°C/Gas Mark 4 and place a small dish containing 100ml water in the bottom. As the water evaporates, it will create a steamy environment in the oven. This keeps the outside of the loaf soft as it expands, allowing the dough to rise further for a lighter texture.

Bake the loaf for about 30 minutes, until it is golden brown and sounds hollow when tapped. Remove from the oven and leave to cool for a few moments while you prepare the icing.

Sift the icing sugar into a bowl and gradually stir in 2–3 tablespoons of hot water until you have an icing that is thin enough to drizzle. Using a spoon, drizzle it over the loaf in random lines. Sprinkle with the crushed hazelnuts, if using. Leave to cool completely before cutting it with a serrated knife into slices 1–2 cm thick.

Chocolate Hazelnut Cake

This cake is made with ground hazelnuts rather than flour, plus a small amount of polenta to give it a better texture, which means it is wheat- and gluten-free. Hazelnuts and chocolate are a wonderful and popular combination. Most of us will have encountered a very seductive chocolate hazelnut spread, launched half a century ago, and further proof of the pairing's success is that noisette eggs are always the first to fly off the Konditor & Cook shelves at Easter time.

This cake tastes best served at room temperature. You can also warm it slightly in a microwave or a low oven for a few minutes. The chocolate topping will soften and, with a little cream on the side, it can be served as a delicious dessert.

Makes a 21cm cake

100g ground hazelnuts

20g polenta

125g unsalted butter

225g dark chocolate (54 per cent cocoa solids), chopped

25ml dark rum (or milk, for a non-alcoholic version)

6 medium eggs, separated

150g caster sugar

For the topping:

25g unsalted butter

50ml single cream

150g dark chocolate (70 per cent cocoa solids), finely chopped

3 tbsp toasted skinned hazelnuts, coarsely crushed (optional)

Start by making the topping, as it needs to cool down and set before you can use it to decorate the cake. Put the butter and cream in a small saucepan and heat almost to boiling point. Add the chocolate, reduce the heat and stir until the chocolate has melted and the mixture is smooth and glossy. Set this ganache aside to cool.

Heat the oven to 165°C/Gas Mark 3. To give the cake a rustic look, you could use the same method to line a 21cm round cake tin as described in the Coffee and Walnut Cake on page 19. Alternatively, butter the tin and line the base with baking parchment.

Mix the ground hazelnuts and polenta together in a bowl. Melt the butter in a small saucepan, then add the chocolate and stir until melted. Mix in the rum or milk and set aside to cool; the mixture should thicken to a creamy consistency.

Put the egg whites in a large, very clean bowl and, using an electric mixer, whisk with a little of the sugar until they reach soft peaks. Gradually beat in the rest of the sugar until you have a soft-peaked meringue. Add the yolks and beat for 4 minutes on medium speed. The long beating prevents the cake from cracking while it is baking.

Continued...

Add the ground hazelnuts and polenta to the chocolate mixture and mix with a spatula. Now gently fold in the eggs. Pour the mixture into the prepared tin and bake for about 40 minutes, until a skewer inserted in the centre comes out clean. Remove the cake from the oven and leave to cool.

To turn the cake out of the tin, loosen the sides first if necessary, then cover the tin with a flat plate, turn them both upside down, lift off the tin and peel the paper off the cake. Place a cake board on the base and turn it back over.

Once the ganache is semi-set, beat it for a few minutes with an electric mixer until it becomes paler and forms stiff peaks (beating some air into it makes it easier to pipe). Transfer it to a piping bag fitted with a number-10 star nozzle and pipe in waves over the cake. As an extra touch, you could sprinkle the coarsely crushed hazelnuts over the top.

Raspberry Chequer Cake

The secret of this cake's chequerboard pattern lies not in using a special tin but in the cutting of the layers and their assembly. Originally we baked this cake to a Victoria sponge recipe but I feel that this is a cake for an occasion, so I have remastered it with references to its distant cousin, the Battenberg. This version is an almond sponge coated in raspberry frosting and finished with white chocolate leaves or chocolate flakes – a cake fit for a special celebration.

Makes a 20cm cake

150g plain flour

1 tsp baking powder

125g ground almonds

250g salted butter, softened

¼ tsp almond extract

250g caster sugar

5 medium eggs, beaten

a little pink food colouring

For the filling and frosting:

150g raspberries

2 tbsp caster sugar

250g mascarpone cheese

350ml double cream

For a festive finish:

50g flaked almonds

200g white chocolate

2 tbsp vegetable oil

about 16 fresh bay leaves

50g raspberries

For a simple finish:

75g white chocolate flakes

50g raspberries

a little icing sugar

Heat the oven to 180°C/Gas Mark 4. Line two 20cm sandwich tins with foil or baking parchment.

Sift the flour and baking powder into a bowl then add the ground almonds. Using an electric mixer on medium speed, beat the butter, almond extract and sugar together for several minutes, until really light and fluffy. Reduce the speed of the mixer and gradually beat in the eggs, alternating them with the flour mixture. Once all the egg has been added, fold in the remaining flour mixture.

Place half the mixture in one of the prepared tins. Add a drop of pink food colouring to the remaining mix and whisk until it is an even pale pink tone (it usually darkens during baking). Transfer the coloured mixture to the second cake tin.

Place both tins in the oven and bake for about 35 minutes, until a skewer inserted in the centre comes out clean. Remove the cakes from the oven and leave to cool in their tins on a wire rack. Turn the cakes out and peel off the backing paper. Using a large, serrated knife, carefully cut each layer in half horizontally, giving you 2 white layers and 2 pink layers.

You will now need a 6cm and a 12cm pastry cutter, or find two glasses or saucers this size. Cut out a 6cm disc from the centre of each sponge layer (you will need to cut round a glass or saucer with a small sharp knife), but leave the disc in position. Next cut out a 12cm circle. Now swap the middle O-rings: a pink one goes into each white sponge and a white one into each pink sponge (see picture on page 40).

Once the sponges are prepared, make the filling and frosting. Place the raspberries in a bowl with the caster sugar and mascarpone and use a spatula to crush and blend the raspberries into the cheese and sugar. Pour in the cream and, using an electric hand beater, whisk to a stiff, mousse-like consistency.

To assemble the cake, place one of the layers on a cake board (it is best to try to push the board under the sponges rather than lifting them up). Let's assume you start with one of the white-edged layers. Spread evenly with about a fifth of the filling, pushing a little in between the rings to bind them together. Carefully place a pink-edged layer on top. Rather than lifting each ring of sponge, try to push a second cake board or flat metal disc under the sponge, then slide it on top of the first layer. Bond and cover with filling as before.

Now repeat the process with the second white-edged sponge and finally the second pink-edged sponge. Using a palette knife, cover the top and sides with the rest of the filling to form an even layer of frosting. The sides should be nice and smooth, as they will be left plain, though the top will be decorated. Place in the fridge to chill while you prepare the final decorations.

If you are doing the festive finish, scatter the almonds over a baking sheet lined with baking parchment and toast for about 4 minutes in an oven heated to 180°C/Gas Mark 4. They should be just turning golden. Remove from the oven and leave to cool.

To make the chocolate leaves, temper the white chocolate following the instructions on page 217. Although you can make them with untempered chocolate, they will be less fragile and set harder with properly tempered chocolate.

Clean the bay leaves by wiping them with a damp tea towel. Turn the leaves underside up and brush lightly with the oil, using a cotton ball or kitchen paper.

Next brush the leaves with the chocolate. Apply a thin coat of chocolate to the underside of each leaf and set them down on a parchment-lined tray. Chill until set, then apply another layer of chocolate and chill again to set. Once the chocolate is hard, carefully peel off the real leaf from the chocolate leaf.

To finish the cake, arrange the leaves around the edge to form a sunflower design, then fill the centre with the raspberries. Press the toasted flaked almonds on the sides of the cake.

For a simpler finish, sprinkle the top and sides of the cake with the white chocolate flakes and then scatter some raspberries among the chocolate on top. Give it a light dusting of icing sugar for a wintry effect.

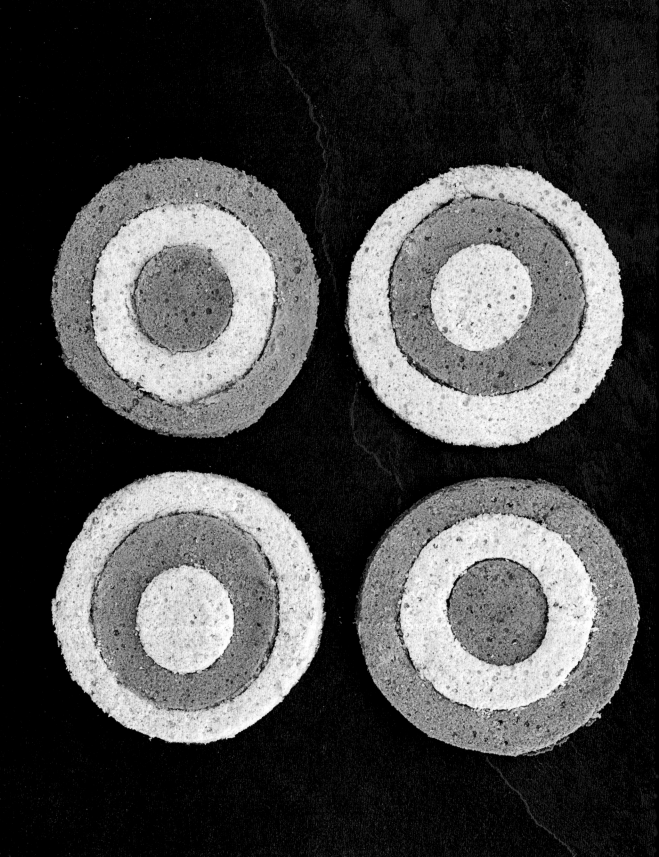

Chocolate Biscuit Cake

This is a brilliant recipe as it requires no baking and can be made really quickly. You just need a little patience while it sets in the fridge. In the early days of Konditor & Cook, this cake became an instant hit. We cheekily labelled it a 'natural anti-depressant', as it was very popular as a pick-me-up snack for tired office workers. I used to say that if my German college teacher could see me he would go nuts: almost up to my elbows in 16 kilos of warm, dark, liquid chocolate mixture – all those years of specialised training to end up wrestling with something as unsophisticated as this. Unsophisticated it may be, but it's utterly delicious and, if you want to have some kitchen fun with your kids, it should appeal to aspiring pastry chefs.

I like to decorate the top with brazil nuts. You could substitute other nuts or leave them off the top altogether.

Makes 1 large loaf

150g unsalted butter

100g golden syrup

200g dark chocolate (54 per cent cocoa solids), chopped

1 medium egg, lightly beaten

330g digestive biscuits (or similar)

60g walnuts

60g sultanas

100g glacé cherries

75g brazil nuts

Line a 23cm square cake tin or similar-sized flat dish with baking parchment. (You could use individual silicone loaf tins to make your own chocolate bars, in which case you will need to break the biscuits up smaller. Or you could use a 20cm x 34cm brownie tin but only fill three-quarters of the tin with biscuit mixture.)

Melt the butter and golden syrup together in a saucepan and then bring to the boil. Add the chocolate, reduce the heat to its lowest setting and stir with a whisk until the chocolate has melted.

Gradually add the beaten egg and continue to stir with the whisk until the mixture has thickened a little and formed a shiny emulsion. The egg will cook in the heat of the mixture but be careful not to let it boil (the temperature shouldn't reach above 85°C). Remove from the heat.

Break up the biscuits into large chunks (quarters are fine), put them in a bowl and add the walnuts, sultanas and half the glacé cherries. Pour the hot chocolate mix over the dry ingredients and mix gently with a wooden spoon. Decant the mixture into the prepared tin, leaving the runny chocolate on the side of the bowl for now. Press the mixture flat in the tin.

Put the brazil nuts in the bowl that contained the chocolate mixture and, using a spatula, coat them in the liquid chocolate from the side of the bowl. Sprinkle them in a loose pattern over the biscuit cake, then place the remaining glacé cherries among them. For an American touch, you could also decorate it with mini marshmallows.

Chill for 3 hours or until set, then cut into bars or long fingers.

Figgy Fruit Loaf
– a Cake for Cheese

An earlier version of this dairy-free, fruit-packed recipe accompanied a trekking tour to the Himalayas, giving the climbers a welcome boost of fructose on their endeavour to climb Mount Everest. This updated version, still dairy free, is bursting with dried fruits and nuts; surprisingly, it makes a brilliant companion to hard cheeses such as artisan Cheddar, Wensleydale or Manchego. Baked in smaller loaf tins, it makes an unusual edible gift.

The loaf can be stored in an airtight container in a cool, dry place for up to 3 months.

Makes 1 large loaf

100g dried figs

100g raisins

juice and grated zest
   of 1 unwaxed lemon

100g dates

100g glacé cherries, halved

100g mixed candied peel,
   chopped

100g walnuts

100g unblanched almonds

3 medium eggs

125g caster sugar

100g self-raising flour

¼ tsp salt

Line a 1kg loaf tin with baking parchment. Remove the hard stalks from the figs and cut the figs into strips. Set aside a few strips for decoration and put the rest in a bowl. Add the raisins, stir in the lemon juice and leave to soak for at least an hour.

Heat the oven to 180°C/Gas Mark 4. Cut the dates in half and set aside a few pieces for decoration. Put the rest of the dates in a bowl, add the glacé cherries, candied peel and lemon zest and mix loosely. Stir in the walnuts, almonds and soaked fruit and mix again.

Briefly whisk the eggs with the sugar, using a fork or hand whisk, to start dissolving the sugar. Add to the fruit and nuts and mix well with a spatula. Add the flour and salt and stir until there are no flour pockets remaining in the mixture, but be careful not to over-mix.

Transfer the mixture to the lined tin and then decorate with the reserved figs and dates.

Bake for 20 minutes, then reduce the heat to 150°C/Gas Mark 2 and bake for a further 30 minutes, until a small knife or wooden toothpick inserted in the centre comes out clean, without any crumbs sticking to it. Remove from the oven and leave to cool in the tin.

To serve, cut into thin slices and use to make cheese sandwiches, or cut into batons and pile them up with cheese wedges on your cheeseboard.

Orange and Lavender Crunch Cake

The culinary use of flowers was something I discovered through having my own small London garden and studying gardening books by the late Geoff Hamilton. I believe the Victorians were pioneers in this field. Around late spring, at the Chelsea Flower Show, we usually bake a few rounds of orange and lavender crunch. I prefer a loaf shape for this, as it bakes a bit higher and the proportion of cake to crunch is better. In essence, this is a pound cake flavoured with orange zest. To give it more moisture and a golden crumb, I recommend using golden caster sugar. After baking, the cake is topped with an orange and lavender crunch made from orange juice infused with lavender flowers.

With its sweet, fragrant nature, this cake makes the perfect tea cake (the broken teacup is optional). A serving of crème fraîche or soured cream on the side makes the perfect partner. If you want to make it into a showstopper, you could decorate it with shards of amber-coloured lavender caramel.

Makes 1 large loaf

200g self-raising flour

200g salted butter, softened

200g golden caster sugar

grated zest of 1 large,
   unwaxed orange

4 medium eggs,
   lightly beaten

For the orange and
lavender crunch:

juice of the orange, above

200g golden caster sugar

2 tsp dried lavender,
   (preferably organic) or
   fresh lavender flowers,
   if in season

For the lavender caramel
shards (optional):

a little vegetable or
   sunflower oil, for
   brushing

200g caster sugar

1 tsp dried or
   fresh lavender

Heat the oven to 180°C/Gas Mark 4. Butter a 900g loaf tin and dust it lightly with flour, or line it with baking parchment.

Sift the flour into a bowl and set aside. Using an electric mixer, beat the softened butter with the sugar and orange zest until light and fluffy. Beat in about a quarter of the beaten eggs, then reduce the speed and add a tablespoon of the flour. Repeat this process until all the egg is mixed in, then gently fold in the remainder of the flour.

Transfer the mixture to the prepared tin and bake for 10 minutes. Reduce the temperature to 165°C/Gas Mark 3 and bake for a further 35 minutes, until a skewer or small knife inserted in the centre comes out clean. (If you find that the top is getting too dark before the cake is done, cover it with a sheet of foil.) Leave to cool in the tin for about an hour, then turn out on to a wire rack.

To make the orange and lavender crunch, mix the orange juice with the sugar, then add the lavender. You should have a spreadable but not too runny paste – adjust the amount of sugar if necessary. Drizzle the mixture down the middle of the cake, either keeping the topping neat or allowing the occasional 'leg' to run down the side for a more home-made look.

Continued...

If you decide to make the lavender caramel shards, line a baking tray with baking parchment and brush with a little oil. Put the sugar in a heavy-based pan with 200ml water and heat gently, stirring occasionally to dissolve the sugar. Bring to the boil and simmer until it turns into an amber caramel; if you have a sugar thermometer, it should register 147.5°C (hard crack is the technical term for this stage). Be warned: you are dealing with very high temperatures and any contact with the hot caramel will cause severe burns. Do not leave the pan unattended.

Add the lavender to the caramel, then pick up the pan using oven gloves and carefully pour the caramel into the prepared baking tray. Leave to cool and set. Brush the caramel with a little oil to prevent it absorbing moisture. Crack it into shards by whacking it gently with a wooden spoon. Stud the cake with the shards.

Chocolate Orange Bundt

In recent years the requests for 'free-from' cakes have greatly increased, with 'free from gluten' being most in demand, but also free from dairy products. I find butter superior in flavour and texture to its cheaper cousin, margarine. But for a cake shop that prides itself on using butter, it is equally important that we have a free-from-lactose recipe in our repertoire with a good texture and depth of flavour.

This chocolate bundt cake certainly delivers. It makes a lovely afternoon-tea cake, especially if baked in one of the ornate bundt tins now available. Simply dust the cake with icing sugar or pipe lines of melted dark chocolate over it.

This recipe can be used as a base for cupcakes or upside-down cakes by adapting the flavourings or changing the tin it is baked in.

Makes a 23cm cake

225ml soya milk

150ml olive oil

75ml sunflower oil

300g caster sugar

4 medium eggs

75g cocoa powder

2 tsp baking powder

250g self-raising flour

grated zest of 1 unwaxed orange

½ tsp crushed cardamom seeds

¼ tsp vanilla extract or seeds of ¼ vanilla pod

To finish (optional):

2 tbsp icing sugar or 100g dark chocolate, melted

Heat the oven to 165°C/Gas Mark 3. Grease and flour a 23cm bundt tin (since this recipe is dairy free, I suggest using sunflower or coconut oil for greasing). Make sure you get into all the corners and details of your tin. Scatter in some plain flour, move it around so all the sides are covered, then turn the tin upside down and shake out the excess flour.

Put all the ingredients into a mixing bowl and beat on high speed with an electric mixer for 5 minutes. Pour into the prepared tin.

Bake for about 50 minutes, until a toothpick or metal skewer inserted in the centre comes out clean. Remove from the oven and leave to cool in the tin for about 30 minutes, then turn out on to a wire rack and leave to cool completely. If the cake sticks to the tin when you turn it out, it sometimes helps to tap the tin with a rolling pin.

Either leave the cake plain to show off the markings of your bundt tin or dust it with the icing sugar; this will also show off the markings and shadows of the tin. Alternatively, put the melted chocolate into a parchment piping bag (see page 216) and pipe randomly in thin lines over the top of the cake.

Tarts and Puddings

Raspberry Fudge Tart

This is a fantastic dessert, combining the sharpness of fruit with the richness of dark chocolate. It is quite easy to make, especially if you have a freezer stocked with some sweet pastry and raspberries. I have suggested two different finishes below: a simple dusting of cocoa powder and an eye-catching and elegant marbled white chocolate pattern.

Serves 8–10

1 quantity of Sweet Pastry
    (see page 206)

75g unsalted butter

300ml double cream

250g dark chocolate
    (54 per cent cocoa
    solids), chopped

200g raspberries

Finish 1:

1 tbsp dark cocoa powder

Finish 2:

75g white chocolate,
    chopped

about 12 fresh raspberries

Roll out the pastry on a lightly floured surface to 3–4mm thick and use to line a 25cm loose-bottomed tart tin. Trim off the excess and chill the pastry case for 30 minutes. Heat the oven to 180°C/Gas Mark 4.

Line the pastry case with aluminium foil, draping it over the edges a little, and fill it with baking beans or rice. Bake blind for 15 minutes, then remove from the oven and leave to stand for 5 minutes. Lift out the foil with the beans or rice and return the pastry case to the oven for 5–10 minutes, until the pastry is golden brown and crisp. Remove from the oven and leave to cool.

To make the filling, melt the butter in a saucepan over a low heat, then add the cream and gently bring to near-boiling point. Add the chopped chocolate and stir until it has completely melted and you have a smooth ganache.

Scatter the raspberries over the base of the tart. Carefully pour in the chocolate ganache and level the top with a palette knife. If you opt for finish 1, refrigerate immediately until firm. Finish 2 should be applied as soon as you have filled the tart with the ganache.

For finish 1, remove the tart from the fridge an hour before serving, place a few 1cm-wide strips of cardboard in an abstract criss-cross pattern across the tart and dust lightly with the cocoa powder. Carefully lift off the cardboard.

Alternatively, for finish 2, melt the white chocolate in a bowl set over a pan of gently simmering water or in a microwave; if using a microwave, be very careful and use a low setting, as white chocolate can burn easily. Make a small parchment piping bag (see page 216), fill it with the melted chocolate, then cut a 1–2mm opening in the tip. Pipe the white chocolate in S shapes over the top of the tart. Using a toothpick or skewer, create some feathered swirls, Florentine-paper style. Chill the tart until ready to serve.

101% Bramley Apple Pie

One way of assessing the quality of a bakery or café is to consider how well it executes a typical regional or national recipe. When I'm eating my way through German cake shops, or *Konditoreien*, I often opt for *Gedeckter Apfelkuchen* (apple pie) or *Käsekuchen* (baked cheesecake). Both are usually on offer and can be pretty good indicators of quality. Are the apples fresh, canned, or dried and reconstituted? Is the cheesecake's pastry made with butter or margarine, the filling moist or bone dry? In the UK I tend to check the quality of the scones or chocolate cake, but apple pie is a fantastic indicator, too.

A lot of 'crimes' are committed in the making of this most basic pie. That is why at Konditor & Cook we went completely the other way with this unadulterated pie. We called it the 101% Bramley Apple Pie (technically, of course, it is not!) to draw attention to the filling, which doesn't contain any thickeners or sweeteners.

The pie gets its character from the fresh sharpness of the apples combined with the sweetness of the pastry. It's really easy to make and, served with cream or ice cream, is the purest of desserts.

Serves 8

1 quantity of Sweet Pastry (see page 206)

800g cooking apples, such as Bramley (about 650g peeled weight)

1½ tbsp semolina (or breadcrumbs or cake crumbs)

1 egg yolk, beaten with 1 tbsp milk

Roll out just over half the pastry on a lightly floured surface to 3–4mm thick. Use to line a 25cm loose-bottomed tart tin, trimming off the excess. Chill for 30 minutes.

Heat the oven to 180°C/Gas Mark 4. Peel and core the apples, then cut them into 2mm-thick slices. You can do this with a knife but a mandoline or food processor will give the best results.

Remove the pastry case from the fridge, sprinkle the base with the semolina to prevent it getting soggy, then pile in the sliced apples, forming a dome in the centre.

Roll out the remaining pastry into a disc large enough to cover the pie and place on top. Press down the edges and trim off the excess pastry. Brush the egg and milk mixture evenly over the top, wait a few minutes, then brush a second time. To add a little decorative element, use the tip of a skewer to etch circles into the pastry or use a fork to create a tartan or trellis design.

Bake the pie for 30–35 minutes, until golden brown. The thin apple slices trapped beneath the pastry lid should be just nicely 'steam cooked' and should give a layered appearance once the pie is cut open. You could check the apples by inserting a small knife; if there is some resistance, then leave the pie for a little longer, perhaps covering the top to stop it becoming too dark. Remove from the oven and leave to cool for 1 hour before serving.

Rhubarb and Orange Meringue

This is based on one of my mother's recipes. Her baking was simple and artisanal, with much depending on what was available from the land. But since then there has been a food revolution. Taste buds expect to be tantalised on more than one level, while ideas about presentation change at a rapid pace. We constantly seek new ways of updating old favourites; discovering ingredients that add a new depth of flavour is what makes baking so exciting.

In this recipe I've retained the traditional yeast-leavened base but given the tart a bit of a lift by adding candied orange zest to the meringue topping. I admit it receives mixed reactions. Some people prefer the richness of a pastry base (if you do, then replace the bun dough with the sweet pastry on page 206), while others love the softness and lightness of the dough, which contains less sugar and fat than pastry. It acts as a taste leveller to the contrasting sharpness of the fruit, while the light meringue further rounds off the flavours, softening the kick of the fruit with caramel sweetness.

The recipe works well with other sharp fruits, such as gooseberries and redcurrants. If using these, I would omit the orange; instead, sprinkle flaked almonds on the uncooked meringue for gooseberries and add vanilla to the meringue for redcurrants.

Serves 12

1 quantity of Bun Dough
  (see page 209)

900g rhubarb, trimmed
  and cut into 1cm lengths

2 tbsp caster sugar

1 quantity of Light
  Meringue (see page 210)

For the candied
orange zest:

75g caster sugar

75ml water

1 unwaxed orange

While the bun dough is rising, put the rhubarb pieces in a bowl, sprinkle with the sugar and set aside.

Grease a 25cm x 40cm baking tray with a little butter. Roll out the dough on a lightly floured surface into a rectangle the size of the baking tray. The dough should be soft, velvety and easy to pick up with your hands in order to transfer it to the baking tray – imagine a pizza chef spinning the dough around in his hands. Line the baking tray with the dough.

Heat the oven to 165°C/Gas Mark 3. Make the meringue. Scatter the rhubarb over the dough. Spoon the meringue on top and use the back of the spoon to give it an undulating surface.

Place in the oven and bake for about 25 minutes, until the meringue is lightly brown and all those lovely caramel flavours have developed. Remove from the oven and leave to cool. The tart is best served cold so you can enjoy the refreshing sharpness of the rhubarb in contrast with the sweetness of the meringue.

To make the candied orange, put the sugar and water in a small pan and bring to the boil, stirring to dissolve the sugar. Peel off the orange zest using a vegetable peeler. With a sharp knife, cut it into 1mm-thick strips, then add to the boiling sugar syrup. Turn down the heat and simmer for 5 minutes. Remove from the heat and fish out the strips of zest. Leave on a piece of baking parchment to cool, then scatter over the tart to decorate. Finish with a light dusting of icing sugar, if you like.

Pink Kick Strawberry and Apple Pie

This pie is a real 'looker'. Not only that, but it surprises with its intriguing flavour combination. Anyone who has ever enjoyed a bowl of fresh strawberries with a delicate dusting of freshly ground white pepper on top knows that the pepper intensifies the strawberries' aroma. In this recipe, pink peppercorns and strawberries give the apples a lovely pink hue and your taste buds a surprise kick. It's delicious served with vanilla ice cream or some pouring cream.

Serves 6–8

1 quantity of Sweet Pastry
    (see page 206)

700g Bramley or Discovery
    apples (about 600g
    prepared weight)

2 tbsp caster sugar

200g strawberries

1 tbsp pink peppercorns

1 tbsp semolina
    (or breadcrumbs)

To finish:

100g apricot glaze (or
    apricot jam, heated and
    strained through a sieve)
    or a little icing sugar

Roll out the pastry on a lightly floured surface to 3–4mm thick and use to line a deep 20cm loose-bottomed tart tin. Trim off the excess pastry and chill the pastry case for 30 minutes. Heat the oven to 180°C/Gas Mark 4.

Line the pastry case with aluminium foil, draping it over the edges a little, and fill it with baking beans or rice. Bake blind for 15 minutes, then remove from the oven and leave to stand for 5 minutes. Lift out the foil with the beans or rice and return the pastry case to the oven for 5 minutes or until it has started to colour slightly. Remove the pastry case from the oven but do not turn the oven off.

Meanwhile, prepare the apples: peel and core them and cut into quarters, then cut them into slices 2–3mm thick. Set aside about 125g of the slices to decorate the pie, sprinkling them with a tablespoon of the sugar. Put the remaining apple slices in a saucepan and mix with the rest of the sugar. Cook over a medium heat for about 10 minutes, stirring occasionally, until the apples are soft and beginning to break up.

Hull the strawberries and cut them into halves or quarters, depending on size. Set aside a quarter of them for decorating the top of the pie. Add the strawberries and pink peppercorns to the apples and cook until the strawberries start to soften. Remove from the heat and leave to cool.

Continued...

Sprinkle the base of the pastry case with the semolina, then fill it with the apple and strawberry mixture. Decorate the top with a slightly overlapping circle of apple slices then fill the centre with the reserved strawberries.

Bake at 180°C/Gas Mark 4 for about 35 minutes, until the pastry is golden brown. Remove from the oven and leave to cool for 15 minutes, then remove the pie from the tin and place on a wire cooling rack.

To finish, either dust with icing sugar or glaze with the apricot jam. Put the glaze or strained jam in a small saucepan and bring to boiling point. If the jam is very thick, you may have to add a little water. Apply the jam with a pastry brush, coating the top of the pie with a thin film. Slow movements, dabbing on the jam, are best, rather than vigorous criss-crossing brushstrokes of watery jam. The pie will set more quickly if it is still a little warm.

Twice-baked Raspberry Ricotta Cheesecake with a Thyme Crust

A little resourcefulness can go a long way in the kitchen, whether it's rustling up a meal from next to nothing in the fridge or substituting one ingredient for another.

At Konditor & Cook, sometimes we need a bit of ingenuity to make a dessert stand out. It might be the way we finish it, the manner in which we present it, or the choice of 'magic' ingredients in the first place. I love to use fresh herbs and flowers in salads, and a few of my favourite sweets also draw on ingredients available in my garden.

With the subtle addition of lemon thyme, I try to infuse this cheesecake with the flavour of an Italian country garden.

Serves 6–8

1 quantity of **Sweet Pastry**
(see page 206)

a sprig of lemon thyme

250g ricotta cheese

3 tbsp plain flour

grated zest of ½ unwaxed
lemon

2 eggs, separated

75ml milk

85g caster sugar

225g raspberries

icing sugar, for dusting

Roll out the pastry on a lightly floured surface to 3–4mm thick. Sprinkle evenly with the leaves from the lemon thyme sprig, then roll flat with the rolling pin. Keeping the pastry herb-side up, use to line a deep 20cm loose-bottomed tart tin, then trim off the excess. Chill for 30 minutes.

Heat the oven to 180°C/Gas Mark 4.

Line the pastry case with aluminium foil, draping it over the edges a little, and fill it with baking beans or rice. Bake blind for 15 minutes, then remove from the oven and leave to stand for 5 minutes. Lift out the foil with the beans or rice and return the pastry case to the oven for 5 minutes or until it has started to colour slightly.

Using a spatula, mix the ricotta with the flour, lemon zest and egg yolks, then add the milk and mix to a smooth, creamy paste.

Put the egg whites in a clean bowl, start whisking, then gradually add the caster sugar and whisk to a soft-peaked meringue. Using a rubber spatula, gently fold the meringue into the ricotta mixture.

Continued...

Pour the mixture into the pastry case and spread evenly with a palette knife or the back of a spoon. Arrange the raspberries on top.

Bake at 180°C/Gas Mark 4 for 10 minutes, then reduce the temperature to 150°C/Gas Mark 2 and bake for a further 20 minutes. The filling should have risen in the centre.

Gently remove from the oven (but do not turn the oven off) and leave for 15 minutes (this stops the filling from rising too much and cracking open, then collapsing). Return to the oven for a final 15 minutes.

Remove from the oven and leave to cool. Dust lightly with icing sugar before serving.

Classic Lemon Tart

This is one of our oldest recipes. It's a classic to get under your belt – or should that be your baker's apron? The recipe appears on our summer cake list and is a firm favourite with many Konditor & Cook customers.

Serves 6

1 quantity of Sweet Pastry
(see page 206)

grated zest of
1 unwaxed lemon

2 eggs

4 egg yolks (the whites will
keep in the fridge for a
week or can be frozen)

140g caster sugar

100ml lemon juice (about
2 lemons)

160ml double cream

1 tbsp icing sugar

Roll out the pastry on a lightly floured surface to 3–4mm thick and use to line a 25cm loose-bottomed tart tin. Trim off the excess pastry and chill the pastry case for 30 minutes. Heat the oven to 180°C/Gas Mark 4.

Line the pastry case with aluminium foil, draping it over the edges a little, and fill it with baking beans or rice. Bake blind for 15 minutes, then remove from the oven and leave to stand for 5 minutes. Lift out the foil with the beans or rice and return the pastry case to the oven for 5 minutes, until light brown. Remove from the oven and set aside. Turn the oven temperature down to 165°C/Gas Mark 3.

Sprinkle the lemon zest over the base of the pastry case. Put the eggs, egg yolks and caster sugar into a bowl and beat briefly using a handheld electric mixer. Add the lemon juice and mix well.

In a separate bowl, very softly whip the double cream until it just starts to thicken but is still quite runny. Whisk the egg and lemon mixture into the cream to form a smooth 'sauce'.

Pour into the pastry case and bake for about 35 minutes, until lightly golden. The tart must not crack on the top, as that is a sign it is overcooked. Leave to cool.

To finish, dust the whole tart with icing sugar just before serving. Alternatively, for a decorative flourish, cut a few strips of cardboard into narrow irregular-sized strips, then lay them in a criss-cross pattern on top of the tart before dusting with icing sugar.

Toffee Apple Crumble

Tucking into a slice of this wonderful spiced and caramel-scented pie is the culinary equivalent of sitting on a soft rug by a smouldering log fire. Its homely, spicy-sweet taste makes it a real autumn and winter warmer. Mind you, I think it's quite all right to serve it with a big scoop of ice cream as a dessert for a sizzling barbecue, too. Toffee is one of those flavours that triggers a lot of people's taste buds and this wonderful, creamy toffee caramel can be used for other desserts – poured over ice cream or warm brownies, for example. It will keep in the fridge for up to 2 weeks.

Serves 6

1 quantity of Sweet Pastry (see page 206)

4 tbsp white breadcrumbs (or sponge cake crumbs)

500g Bramley, Discovery or Russet apples (about 420g prepared weight), peeled, cored and thinly sliced

½ quantity of Streusel (see page 208), with 1 tsp ground mixed spice added

1 tbsp icing sugar

For the toffee caramel:

100g unsalted butter

150g caster sugar

50ml single cream

Roll out the pastry on a lightly floured surface to 3–4mm thick and use to line a deep 20cm loose-bottomed tart tin. Trim off the excess and chill the pastry case for 30 minutes. Heat the oven to 200°C/Gas Mark 6.

Sprinkle the breadcrumbs over the base of the pastry case, layer the sliced apples on top, then scatter over the streusel mix. Bake for 35 minutes, until the crumble is lightly browned and the apples are tender.

While the pie is in the oven, make the toffee caramel. You will need a small, heavy-based pan. When the caramel is ready, it's important to cool the pan quickly, so fill the kitchen sink, or a heatproof container large enough to take the base of the pan, with cold water in readiness.

Put the butter in the heavy-based pan and place over a medium heat until it is just below simmering. Add the sugar and stir until dissolved. Cook over a low heat until caramelised; it should be the colour of brown eggshells.

Pour in the cream in a slow stream. The mixture will bubble up and be very, very hot, so it's a good idea to be extra careful and perhaps make sure your arms are covered. Briefly continue to stir over the heat until the caramel forms a smooth emulsion. Now dip the base of the pan in the cold water to prevent the caramel darkening further. Set aside.

Remove the pie from the oven and leave to cool on a wire rack. Lift it out of the tin and dust with the icing sugar, then drizzle with the toffee caramel.

Strawboffee Pie

Strawboffee pie is summer's answer to banoffee pie. And once you have mastered this easy recipe, you will hold the key to both these gorgeously seductive puddings from our repertoire.

Our point-of-sale sign for this pudding reads 'simply orgasmic', and with these words summarises the seductive combination of four simple components: sweet biscuit base, caramel toffee, soft cream and fresh fruitiness.

Boiling the condensed milk is best done a day in advance but you can do several cans at once and keep them in the cupboard... the rest is as easy as pie!

Serves 8–10

397g can of condensed milk
350ml double cream
350g strawberries, hulled

For the biscuit base:

250g digestive biscuits
125g unsalted butter

Place the unopened can of condensed milk in a large saucepan and cover completely with water, making sure it comes at least 1cm above the top of the can (it is more efficient to do several cans at the same time, thus filling the saucepan). Cover the pan, bring to the boil, then reduce the heat and simmer gently for 4 hours, topping up regularly with water to keep the can covered. Remove from the heat and leave to cool in the water.

Line the base of a 25cm loose-bottomed tart tin with a double layer of cling film. Put the biscuits in a bowl or a plastic bag and crush them to small crumbs using the end of a rolling pin; alternatively, you could whizz them in a food processor.

Melt the butter in a pan, remove from the heat and add the crumbs. Stir until they are evenly coated in the butter.

Spoon the mixture into the lined tin, distribute evenly, then cover with another sheet of cling film and press flat with the back of a spoon. Use your fingertips to make sure the edges are well pressed down. Chill in the fridge or freezer for about an hour, until firm.

Continued...

Using an electric mixer or hand whisk, whip the cream until it forms soft peaks. Be careful not to over-whip to full stiffness, as this would greatly affect texture, flavour and enjoyment.

Now assemble the pie. Remove the base from the fridge or freezer, take off the top layer of cling film, then carefully lift the base out of the tin and peel away the bottom layer of cling film. Place on a dish with a flat surface (otherwise it may break). Using a palette knife or a large spoon, spread with the condensed milk – you might need only three-quarters of the can; it's very rich and sweet and you can tailor the amount to your preference.

Spread the soft whipped cream on top, then arrange the strawberries over it. Small ones can be left whole; larger ones are better quartered and stuck in the cream pointing upwards to give dynamic visual appeal. You can keep the pie in the fridge but it's best enjoyed on the day.

Apple Strudel

I was born in Freiburg and grew up in Baden, an area that belonged to the Austrian Habsburg Empire many generations ago, so it's perhaps not surprising that apple strudel features high on the list of cakes I like to bake at home.

Austria is not only the birthplace of the Sachertorte but also the undisputed home of wonderful *Mehlspeisen* (dishes made with flour), including *Apfelstrudel*.

Serves 6

1kg apples
(Bramley or Discovery)

4 tbsp crème fraîche

2 tbsp sultanas

30g unsalted butter

50g white breadcrumbs
(or cake crumbs)

50g caster sugar

½ tsp ground cinnamon

50g walnuts, chopped

For the strudel pastry:

125g plain flour

1 egg, separated

50ml warm water

1 tsp white vinegar

a pinch of salt

1 tbsp sunflower
or vegetable oil

1 tbsp milk

20g unsalted
butter, melted

To decorate:

2 tbsp caster sugar

½ tsp ground cinnamon

First make the strudel pastry. Sift the flour into a bowl, add all the remaining ingredients except the egg yolk, milk and melted butter, and knead into a smooth, soft dough. Cover with cling film and leave to rest at room temperature for at least an hour.

Meanwhile, prepare the filling. Peel, core and thinly slice the apples. Mix with the crème fraîche and sultanas and set aside. Melt the butter in a frying pan, add the breadcrumbs and fry lightly until the butter releases its aroma, then set aside. Combine the caster sugar and cinnamon and set aside. Heat the oven to 180°C/Gas Mark 4.

On a lightly floured surface, roll the dough out to the size of an A4 sheet of paper. Add more flour to the rolling pin or the surface if you find it is starting to stick. Then dust a large, clean tea towel well with flour, place the dough on top and pull it out into a sheet twice its size (A3). The pastry will appear translucent in places. It is the less translucent areas that you have to pull carefully. Dust your hands with flour and put one hand under the pastry to lift and stretch it – a little bit like a pizza baker would except very low down and very gingerly.

Leaving a 4cm border clear all round, sprinkle the sugar and cinnamon mixture over the pastry, then the walnuts and finally the breadcrumbs.

Continued...

If your tea towel is aligned 'landscape' on your work surface, spread the apple mix over the left half of the sheet, leaving the edges clear. Standing slightly sideways, pick up the end of the tea towel where the apple is and roll it to the right, thus letting the strudel naturally roll itself up. Tuck the ends under.

Place the strudel on a baking tray lined with baking parchment. Mix the egg yolk with the milk and brush it over the strudel with a pastry brush, being careful not to rip any holes in the pastry.

Bake for 35 minutes or until golden brown, brushing the strudel with some of the melted butter halfway through.

Remove the strudel from the oven, brush with more melted butter, then mix together the sugar and cinnamon and sprinkle them over the strudel. Serve with a dollop of soft whipped cream or custard (see page 214).

Melon and Ginger Zinger

Dark, chilly winter days make everyone cry out for comfort food, and there's no denying that people tend to eat less cake in the summer months. This provides a challenge for us bakers. We try to meet it by baking with fresh fruit such as peaches, apricots and plums, all of which would be very successful as a topping for this tray bake. However, we thought that the combination of melon and ginger with some zesty lemon made an almost cooling slice, perfect for hot summer days. Serve with ice cream, if you wish.

Serves 12

1 quantity of Sweet Pastry (see page 206)

2 quantities of Almond Cream (see page 210), with the grated zest of 1 unwaxed lemon added

1 small Galia melon

9 bulbs of stem ginger in syrup (about 125g)

juice of 1 lemon

Roll out the pastry on a lightly floured surface to 3–4mm thick and use to line a 30cm x 38cm baking tray (or a 30cm square cake tin). Trim off the excess pastry and chill the pastry base for 30 minutes.

Spread the almond cream over the pastry base and return it to the fridge for 30 minutes. Heat the oven to 180°C/Gas Mark 4.

Top and tail the melon, then place it upright on a chopping board so that it can't roll around. Using a small paring knife, cut the skin off, going from top to bottom. Place the melon sideways on the board and cut through the middle. Galia melons are quite round, so you can cut either way. Now remove and discard the seeds, place the melon halves on the board and cut each half into at least 12 slices.

Drain excess syrup from the ginger and chop it into small pieces (sprinkling a little of the lemon juice over it helps stop it sticking).

Remove the pastry case from the fridge, sprinkle the ginger over the almond cream and cover the top with the melon pieces. You can do this in a random, rustic fashion or arrange them in a pattern. What is important is that there should be a bit of melon and a bit of ginger in every bite.

Place in the oven and bake for 40–45 minutes, until the pastry is golden brown and the almond cream is set. Remove from the oven and leave to cool a little.

While the tart is still slightly warm, drizzle the remaining lemon juice over the top. Cut into slices and serve.

Summer Pudding Sandwiches

From Glyndebourne to Ascot, no English summer menu is complete without a summer pudding. It is normally moulded in a pudding basin but I think these little sandwiches are great for a summer buffet. Each guest can pick as many triangles as they like, and you don't need a special basin to set them in. Ideally a summer pudding is made from a glut of fresh fruit. To get all the soft fruit at the same time is quite a rarity, but frozen fruit works just as well.

Makes 16 small sandwiches

1 good-quality thinly sliced white sandwich loaf (you will need 8 slices)

fresh fruit or mint leaves, to serve (optional)

For the fruit mix:

700g frozen red berry mix (or, if using fresh fruit, 200g strawberries 200g raspberries, 200g redcurrants, 100g blackcurrants)

150g caster sugar

juice of ½ lemon

200g strawberries, hulled and cut in half

Put all the fruit except the strawberries in a large saucepan with the sugar and lemon juice and heat gently, stirring occasionally to dissolve the sugar. When the mixture starts to simmer, add the strawberries and cook gently for 5 minutes.

Meanwhile, using a serrated knife, trim the crusts off the bread. Remove the fruit mixture from the heat and strain through a sieve to separate the fruit and the juice.

Take 4 pieces of cling film, each large enough to wrap up a sandwich and line them up on a work surface. Dip a slice of bread into the juice and place in the centre of a piece of cling film. Repeat with 3 more slices of bread.

Now divide the fruit between the juice-soaked slices of bread, making sure it covers them completely and flattening it slightly (if you have a little fruit left, you could serve it on the side later). Dip the remaining slices of bread in the juice and place on top to make sandwiches.

Pour any remaining juice over the sandwiches, then wrap the cling film tightly around each one. Place them close together on a chopping board or a small baking tray, cover with another board or tray and add a weight, such as a bottle of wine, to press them down. Leave in the fridge for at least 4 hours or overnight.

To serve, remove the sandwiches from the fridge and unwrap them. Re-trim the edges if necessary, then cut them into fingers or triangles. Present them standing upright on a plate. If you like, you could garnish with any remaining fruit compote, fresh fruit or a few mint leaves. A jug of double cream on the side is a must.

Plum Crumble (*Zwetschgen* Streusel)

It is at Christmas that our recipe list for the shops contains the most German influences. However, in summer we bake this staple recipe using fresh plums. If you have ever travelled to southern Germany in the summer you will have come across this tart or tray bake. Every *Konditorei* (pastry shop) in the land prides itself on baking the best, and it's quite a sport to go round finding your favourite. Imagine a sunny day, the terrace of a café filled to the gunnels, with most of the customers enjoying a portion of their beloved *Zwetschgenkuchen*, cake fork at the ready. Of course, a big helping of *Schlagsahne* (whipped cream) on top is a must. And it helps to hold on to the café menu in order to fend off the wasps, which usually buzz with equal excitement.

I said southern Germany because the town that lends these plums its name, Bühl, is nestled in the foothills of the Black Forest. *Bühler Zwetschgen* is a purple subspecies of the rounder plum. The closest in the UK is the Victoria plum, which is paler and a bit sharper.

There is room for expression when it comes to the topping of the plums. Purists prefer to sprinkle them with cinnamon sugar, others add slivered almonds. My favourite is a cinnamon crumble.

Serves 12–16

1kg plums (Victoria or similar small plums)

2 tbsp caster sugar

¼ tsp ground cinnamon

1 quantity of Bun Dough (see page 209)

½ quantity of Streusel (see page 208)

Cut the plums in half, discard the stones, then cut the fruit into quarters. Mix the sugar with the cinnamon. Place the plums in a bowl and sprinkle with the cinnamon sugar.

Grease a 30cm x 40cm baking tray with a little butter. On a lightly floured surface, roll the bun dough into a rectangle the size of the baking tray, then use to line the tray.

Arrange the plum quarters on the dough in slightly overlapping rows. Sprinkle evenly with the streusel, then leave to prove for 20–30 minutes. Meanwhile, heat the oven to 180°C/Gas Mark 4.

Bake for about 35 minutes, until the crumble is cooked and the dough is turning golden brown. Remove from the oven and leave to cool. If the plums are very sharp, you could dust with a little icing sugar just before serving, or mix a little more cinnamon sugar and sprinkle it over the top.

Prune and Orange Puff Tart with Orange Liqueur Glaze

The great advantage of puff pastry is that you can roll it out very thinly, giving a light base that can be topped with great flavours. You could also use Sweet Pastry here (see page 206). It will make a nice tart but will be very different in character.

A few years back, one of the most passionate home bakers I know, my friend Eva Rothenhoefer, spent a day in one of our kitchens, swapping notes and tips with pastry chef Jonny White. Soon each wanted to create their own version of the best almond and puff pastry tart.

Eva made a luxurious tart topped with almond cream and grated high-quality marzipan, then finished with ripe apricot halves. But Jonny's version, featuring orange zest, prunes and a Cointreau glaze, won the day and has tantalised my taste buds ever since. I love serving it at Christmas. It can be frozen, unglazed, for up to 2 months.

Serves 6–8

250g puff pastry
(see page 207, or use a good-quality bought puff pastry)

1 quantity of Almond Cream (see page 210), with the finely grated zest of 1 unwaxed orange mixed in

250g prunes, pitted and halved

a little icing sugar (optional)

For the glaze:

100g apricot glaze (or apricot jam, heated and strained through a fine sieve)

25ml orange liqueur, such as Cointreau or Grand Marnier

Grease a 25cm loose-bottomed tart tin with a little butter. Roll out the pastry on a lightly floured surface to about 2mm thick and use to line the tin, trimming off the excess. Chill for about 30 minutes. Heat the oven to 190°C/Gas Mark 5.

Using a large spoon or a palette knife, spread the almond cream over the pastry base. Arrange the prune halves in circles over the top. Bake for about 25 minutes, until golden brown. Remove from the oven and leave to cool, then turn the tart out of the tin.

For a rustic look, you can leave the tart as it is or dust it with a little icing sugar. For a festive finish, it is best to glaze it. Heat the glaze or jam in a saucepan, then stir in the orange liqueur. Carefully glaze the top of the tart, using a pastry brush.

Mini Bakes

Lemon Daisy Cakes

These dainty little square cakes are easy to achieve and can be made quickly in large quantities for a special occasion or a cake and bake sale. They were the forerunners to the hugely popular Konditor & Cook Magic Cakes (see page 166). Because the sides aren't covered with icing, they should be eaten within 2 days. They are, though, a good way to practise baking and cutting Magic Cakes.

    The cake is a straightforward sponge flavoured with lemon zest and brushed with lemon juice. The slab is covered in a simple lemon icing, left to set, then divided into squares and decorated with iced daisies. To form a little contrast between the petals, and in reference to the cake's citrussy taste, I add a touch of lime-green food colouring to the lemon icing.

Makes 25

For the lemon sponge:

200g self-raising flour

200g salted butter, softened

200g caster sugar

grated zest of 2 unwaxed lemons

4 medium eggs, lightly beaten

juice of 1½ lemons

For the lemon icing:

250g icing sugar, sifted

juice of ½ lemon

lime-green food colouring (optional)

For the decoration:

1 quantity of Royal Icing (see page 211)

a little yellow food colouring or some mimosa cake sprinkles

Heat the oven to 180°C/Gas Mark 4. Line a 22cm square cake tin with baking parchment.

Sift the flour into a bowl and set aside. Using an electric mixer, beat the softened butter with the caster sugar and lemon zest for about 3 minutes, until light and fluffy.

Beat in about a fifth of the beaten egg, then reduce the speed of the mixer and add 2 tablespoons of the flour. Repeat this process until all the egg is mixed in, then gently fold in the remainder of the flour.

Transfer the mixture to the prepared tin. Bake for 10 minutes, then reduce the temperature to 165°C/Gas Mark 3 and bake for about 30 minutes longer, until a skewer inserted in the centre comes out clean. Leave to cool in the tin for about an hour, then turn out on to a wire rack to cool completely.

To make the lemon icing, sift the icing sugar into a small bowl and gradually add the lemon juice until you have a thick but spreadable mixture. Mix in a little food colouring, if you like, until you have the desired shade.

Turn the cake upside down, peel off the baking parchment and brush or drizzle with the lemon juice. Spread the lemon icing evenly over the surface, using a palette knife. Leave to set for 30 minutes.

Continued...

You now need to divide the slab into 4cm squares. For a 22cm tin, this means cutting it 5 x 5 after trimming off the edges. For accuracy, it is best to place a ruler on the side of the slab and make little indents with a knife along the edges. Allow for the trimmings, then mark every 4cm. When you are happy with your division, cut the cake into squares using a sharp serrated knife. Clean and wipe the knife between cuts. You can leave the cakes as they are or place them in paper cake cases.

Put the royal icing into a parchment piping bag (see page 216) and use to pipe a daisy design on each cake. Add a little yellow food colouring to the royal icing to make the flowers' centres, or use mimosa cake sprinkles as an alternative.

Rainbow Daisy Cakes

You can create more vibrant designs by adding a variety of colours to the lemon icing. For multiple colours, it is best to cut the slab into strips before spreading the icing on – i.e. for 5 colours, cut it into 5 strips. Divide the icing between 5 small glasses and add colourings to create a rainbow effect – for example, red, orange, yellow, green and blue.

Ice each strip of sponge with one of the colours. Leave to set, then cut into little squares, trimming off any icing that dripped down the sides. Decorate as before, or keep them simple and arrange in a rainbow pattern.

Cinnamon Stars

In Germany it is traditional to bake a vast selection of small cookies or petits fours for Christmas. The collective noun for these depends on the geographic location; from *Plätzchen* to *Zuckerbrötle*, every German has fond memories of their favourite.

Cinnamon stars are one of the hardest to get right, and some people happily mix professionally baked ones into their home-made selection. The best recipes are based on a pastry made with almonds as the main ingredient. On top of this pastry sits a thin layer of meringue. This makes the stars quite hard to cut out unless you have a special 'klipp-klapp' cutter.

Here I have used a regular 3cm star cutter and suggested a few tricks to remove the cookies from the cutter. Even without the specialist cutter, it is possible to cut out perfect stars. As a last resort, you could even brush the stars with the meringue after, rather than before, cutting them out.

Makes about 50

2 medium egg whites

a pinch of salt

1 tbsp lemon juice

250g icing sugar, sifted

grated zest of
½ unwaxed lemon

175g ground almonds,
plus extra for rolling

75g mixed candied peel,
whizzed briefly in a food
processor or very
finely chopped

2 tsp ground cinnamon

¼ tsp ground cloves

Put the egg whites in a very clean mixing bowl, add the salt and lemon juice and start beating with an electric mixer. Once you see bubbles forming, gradually add the icing sugar, beating until you have a thick meringue. Transfer about a third of the meringue (125g) to a bowl and set aside, covered with cling film.

Add all the rest of the ingredients to the remaining meringue and mix with a wooden spoon or a spatula to form a firm dough. Dust a work surface lightly with ground almonds and roll out the dough to a sheet 8mm thick. Transfer it to a baking sheet or chopping board that will fit in your fridge.

Using a palette knife, spread a thin, even layer of the reserved meringue on top. You probably won't need it all. What is left can be recycled in a second round of rolling. Chill the sheet in the fridge for 1–2 hours, until the meringue has set and is no longer wet.

Remove the dough from the fridge and cut out stars with a 3cm star-shaped cutter – or a 5cm klipp-klapp cutter, if you happen to have one. Cut the stars out with minimal gaps, as the first round of rolling makes the nicest cookies. For the best results, dip the cutter into cold water first, shake off the excess water, then cut out the star. Use your middle or index finger to push the star upwards out of the cutter, being careful not to get any fingerprints on the delicate meringue surface. Place the cookies 1cm apart on a baking tray lined with baking parchment.

Continued...

Recycle the offcuts by gathering them up and adding some more ground almonds to them, since the meringue on top will have made the dough softer. Roll out, cover with a thin layer of meringue and chill as before, then cut out more stars. If you run out of meringue, you can also bake the stars plain, leave them to cool and then drizzle some melted chocolate over them, or dip them in the Chocolate Icing on page 213.

The baking of the stars is crucial to their success. Since all ovens have their own idiosyncrasies, you may need to adjust the instructions below.

Heat the oven to 200°C/Gas Mark 6. Put the stars on the lowest shelf, as they need hardly any top heat, and bake for about 7 minutes. The meringue should stay nice and white, with a hint of light browning around the edges, the base should be dry and a light golden brown, while the centre should still be moist. Remove from the oven and leave to cool on the tray. Stored in an airtight tin, the stars will keep for several weeks.

Hollywood Dream Cookies

In my family, baking runs in the blood. My grandmother had a large oven on her farm, where she was able to bake 12 massive loaves of bread at once. My mother was a great home baker, and my sister eventually married the village baker – my subsequent holiday job turned into a lifetime of baking.

Unknown to me for a long time, my great-great-aunt Irma was also an excellent baker. She took her baking skills to California, where she ended up working for Hollywood legend Ginger Rogers. In her autobiography, Ms Rogers mentions the wonderful cookies that Irma used to bake for her. There was quite a bit of drama in the perfomer's life and I'm sure Irma kept her nice and sweet with her baking.

Sadly, the recipe has not survived. However, I hope I have created a fantabulous recipe here, befitting a Hollywood star. Fragrant stem ginger, zesty orange and chunks of white chocolate – just the thought of these fabulous ingredients makes me feel as if I'm being spun round on the dance floor in the arms of Fred Astaire.

Makes 24

125g salted butter, softened

100g caster sugar

grated zest of
1 unwaxed orange

1 medium egg yolk

150g self-raising flour

½ tsp bicarbonate of soda

150g white chocolate, chopped

60g stem ginger in syrup, chopped

Put the butter, sugar and orange zest in a mixing bowl and beat with an electric handheld beater on slow speed for 1 minute. Add the egg yolk and beat for about 30 seconds longer.

Sift in the flour and bicarbonate of soda and work everything together into a dough, using a wooden spoon. Stir in the white chocolate and the stem ginger.

Divide the dough in half, shape each piece into a rough log and cut into 12 equal pieces. Roll them into balls and chill for 1 hour.

Heat the oven to 180°C/Gas Mark 4. Grease a baking tray or line it with baking parchment and place the balls of dough on it, pressing them down slightly. Be sure to space them well apart, as they will double in size.

Bake in the top half of the oven for 9–10 minutes. The cookies should develop a golden edge but still be slightly soft in the centre. Remove from the oven and leave to cool. If you don't want to bake all the cookies at once, you can keep the dough balls in the fridge, wrapped in cling film, for up to 5 days; alternatively, freeze them for up to 2 months.

Lavender Shortbread

Preparing little individual treats for afternoon tea or a plate of after-dinner sweets doesn't have to involve special equipment or techniques. These little shortbreads delight with their simplicity but pull big punches in the flavour department. You can cut them into dainty petticoat tails or use a flower cutter to continue the floral theme.

If you fancy elaborating them, use a little raspberry jam to stick a blueberry on to each biscuit. Or make them into sweet canapés by piping a small blob of clotted cream or whipped double cream in the centre of each one and topping with a blueberry. In this case, don't dust them with caster sugar or the cream won't stick.

Makes about 36

1 quantity of Butter
  Shortbread dough
  (see page 208)

2 tsp finely chopped
  dried lavender

3 tbsp caster sugar
  (or Lavender Sugar,
  see page 210)

Heat the oven to 180°C/Gas Mark 4. Follow the Butter Shortbread recipe on page 208, adding the 2 teaspoons of lavender to it and mixing until it comes together into a firm dough.

On a lightly floured surface, roll out the dough to about 6mm thick. I use 2 cake dowels as height markers (see Mocha Swirls, page 101, for the technique). Using a flower-shaped cutter approximately 4cm in diameter, cut out the biscuits.

Place the biscuits 1cm apart on a baking sheet lined with baking parchment and bake for about 14 minutes, until they turn a very light brown (if you use a smaller cutter, reduce the baking time by 1–2 minutes).

Remove from the oven and leave to cool for a few minutes, then sprinkle with the caster sugar or lavender sugar and leave to cool completely. The biscuits will keep in an airtight container for up to a month.

Jammilicious Linzers

Linzer Torte is one of the most popular recipes in southern Germany. It is always baked around Christmas time and in Baden, where I come from, it also forms part of something called *Hochzeitsbrot* (wedding bread), as does the Nusszopf on page 32. It's not really a bread, nor is it actually eaten at weddings (who says the Germans don't have a sense of humour?). Instead it is given to those who aren't invited to the official celebrations but somehow shouldn't be ignored either – distant relatives, neighbours, business associates and so on.

Every *Hausfrau* is proud of her recipe and, of course, thinks it is the best, a bit like the Victoria sponge in the UK. My mother used to add a splash of kirsch to hers. Here I have created a cookie based on the *Linzer Torte* – a sort of bite-sized version. These are, in fact, a tribute to designer Jamie Wieck, creator of the wonderful patterns used throughout this book.

If you can't find ground walnuts, use a coffee grinder or food processor to break them down, or you could substitute ground hazelnuts.

Makes about 32

50g caster sugar

60g salted butter, chilled and diced

1 tbsp milk, plus extra for brushing

1 tsp cocoa powder

1 tsp ground cinnamon

½ tsp ground cloves

a pinch of nutmeg

50g walnuts, finely ground

90g plain flour

150g good-quality raspberry jam

icing sugar, for dusting

Put all the ingredients except the walnuts, flour and raspberry jam into a bowl and mix with a wooden spoon until the butter starts to break up. Mix in the ground walnuts, then sift in the flour and mix that in too. (Alternatively, you could use a freestanding electric mixer fitted with the paddle attachment.) Wrap the dough in cling film and chill for 1 hour. Heat the oven to 180°C/Gas Mark 4.

Remove the dough from the fridge and knead briefly by hand to make it more pliable. Roll it out on a lightly floured surface to about 3mm thick. Using a 3–4cm plain or crinkled square cutter, cut the dough into squares. Re-roll the trimmings to make more (a few offcuts will be useful to add to the baking tray to test the bake).

Place two-thirds of the squares on a greased or parchment-lined baking tray, 1cm apart. Cut the remaining squares in half diagonally and add them to the baking tray. Bake for 10 minutes. Since this dough is quite dark, it is a little harder to tell when it is cooked – place a few offcuts on the tray as testers, so you can remove them and check that they are firm and baked underneath. Remove from the oven and leave to cool for a few minutes.

Warm the raspberry jam in a small pan or a microwave, then pass through a sieve to remove the seeds. Put the jam in a small parchment piping bag fitted with a 3mm nozzle (see page 216) and pipe it over the squares, keeping it 1mm away from the edges.

Dust half the triangles with icing sugar and then, using all the triangles, place one on each biscuit, so that only half of each biscuit is covered and the other half shows the jam. Arrange the biscuits in a pattern on a serving dish.

Raspberry Rock Meringues

If you do a lot of baking, you may end up with a surplus of egg whites, and meringues or macaroons are the easiest way to use them up. These are made with cooked meringue, where the ingredients are heated first, which gives them the advantage of keeping really well. Just make sure you store the meringues in a dry place away from strong smells, preferably in an airtight container.

Plain meringue can be piped into meringue baskets, mini swirls or hearts – all very handy when it comes to rustling up a quick dessert or a treat for a tea party. With raspberries baked in, you have the base for an instant Eton Mess – just add cream. Of course, they are also very pretty on their own.

Makes about 20

4 medium egg whites

240g caster sugar

a pinch of salt

a little pink food colouring

60g fresh or frozen raspberries

Heat the oven to 100°C/Gas Mark ¼. Line a baking tray with baking parchment.

As always with meringues, you need a spotlessly clean bowl without any traces of fat residue. Rinse your bowl out with hot water, then with cold, and dry with kitchen paper. If you have a gas hob, you can heat the egg whites, sugar and salt in a stainless steel mixing bowl (for example, the bowl from a freestanding electric mixer) directly over the flame. Otherwise, put them in a medium saucepan. Place over a medium heat and keep them constantly in motion, using a hand whisk. At first, the mixture will appear quite gloopy, but as it heats it will become thinner.

Remove from the heat once the mixture reaches 55°C. If you don't have a thermometer, test by removing the bowl or pan from the heat and dipping the side of your little finger lightly into the mix. It should feel warm to hot but not scalding hot (if it is, you will be looking at a bowl of scrambled egg whites). Now use an electric hand mixer or a freestanding electric mixer to beat the whites and sugar until light and fluffy.

Mix in a little pink food colouring to give the meringues an appetising appearance. Without any colouring, they will look grey, with pinkish-violet streaks, because the fresh, natural colour of the raspberries will change in the oven. If you use paste colour, dissolve it in a little meringue first; liquid colour can be added directly. Remember that after the meringue has dried in the oven, the colour will be stronger. Break up the raspberries and fold them into the mixture.

Using a tablespoon dipped in cold water, scoop out egg-shaped blobs of meringue and place them 4cm apart on the parchment-lined baking tray. Bake for 1½–2 hours, until the meringues are dry on the outside with a soft centre. Remove from the oven and leave to cool.

Mocha Swirls

In London, traditional afternoon tea has seen a renaissance in recent years. The Berkeley Hotel in Knightsbridge serves a fashion tea, with biscuits and pastries inspired by the world of couture, while at the Corinthia, near the Embankment, they specialise in classics with a modern twist.

With Konditor & Cook's close proximity to Tate Modern and my love for modern art, in the past we have sought inspiration from such artists as Richard Long, Yayoi Kusama, Bridget Riley and my teenage hero, Victor Vasarely. One of my dreams is to set up a Pop Art pop-up cake shop, with all the cakes and pastries inspired by art. These Op Art Mocha Swirls, made from two types of sablé pastry, would definitely feature.

I have come up with a handy trick to make rolling out this pastry very easy; indeed you can use the same method when rolling out pastry for tartlet cases too. If you end up with fewer spirals first time round, don't worry; they will improve with a little practice.

Left unfilled, these cookies will keep in a biscuit tin for up to 2 months. You can also freeze the made-up spiral logs, then cut and bake them at a later date.

Makes about 48 sandwiched cookies

1 quantity of vanilla Sablé Pastry (see page 206)

1 quantity of chocolate Sablé Pastry (see page 206)

1 quantity of Mascarpone Frosting (see page 213), flavoured with coffee

Chill the pastry for an hour, then remove from the fridge and lightly knead each one to make it pliable. This is best done by hand, although it does require a bit of force. To roll the pastry thinly yet evenly (important for an accurate bake), I use a very low-tech gadget – two 25cm-long wooden barbecue skewers. Their diameter is about the thickness I want for the pastry. Start rolling out the vanilla pastry on a lightly floured surface in the usual way but, as it gets thinner, place the skewers on either side to act as markers. Roll the pastry to the same thickness as the skewers; it should be roughly 20cm square. Repeat with the chocolate pastry.

Brush the vanilla sheet with a very little water and put the chocolate sheet on top, then place the skewers either side and roll it out into a square again, ending up with a sheet double the size.

Continued...

Brush with a very little water, just enough to moisten the surface and make it stick, then roll up the pastry towards you to form a cylinder. Do this slowly and tightly, making sure there is no air trapped between the layers. Firm it up by rolling it back and forth until it is about 3cm in diameter. Wrap in cling film and return to the fridge. Heat the oven to 200°C/Gas Mark 6.

Once the log is well chilled and firm, remove from the fridge and cut into 3mm-thick discs with a sharp knife. Place them about 1cm apart on a parchment-lined baking tray. Bake for 8–10 minutes, until golden. Since they are cut so thinly, you have to watch them very closely towards the end. Remove from the oven and leave to cool on the tray.

To fill the biscuits, put the frosting in a piping bag fitted with a 5mm star nozzle, turn half the biscuits upside down and pipe a swirl of the filling on top, keeping it just short of the edge. Place another biscuit on top of each one and push down gently to attach the biscuit and get the filling to line up with the edge. Place in the fridge to set.

Dainty Strawberry Tarts

With the Wimbledon tennis tournament comes the 'official' strawberry season at Konditor & Cook, and these dainty strawberry and orange tarts are a frivolous, melt-in-your-mouth affair.

The blind-baked pastry cases, here, will keep for a month once baked dry and stored in an airtight tin. They are a good standby for when you want to rustle up a quick dessert or sweet treat.

As an alternative to the orange curd, you could fill these tarts with clotted cream or thick-set double cream and top them with your favourite soft fruits; raspberries, blueberries and blackberries all work well.

Makes 24

1 quantity of Sweet Pastry
  (see page 206)

1 quantity of Orange Curd
  (see page 214)

50g apricot glaze
  (or apricot jam, heated
  and strained through a
  sieve)

24 small strawberries

Grease two 12-hole 5cm mini-muffin tins with a little butter. Roll out the pastry on a lightly floured surface to 3mm thick and, using a 6.5cm fluted cutter, cut out small circles. Use them to line the tins, carefully pressing the pastry right down into the base. Chill for 30 minutes. Heat the oven to 180°C/Gas Mark 4.

Line each tartlet case with foil and fill with beans or rice to bake blind. Bake for 15 minutes, then remove from the oven, lift off the foil and beans or rice and return to the oven for about 5 minutes, until golden. Remove from the oven and leave to cool.

Pipe or spoon a heaped teaspoon of orange curd into each tartlet.

Put the glaze or strained jam in a small saucepan and bring to boiling point, then remove from the heat – be careful, as it can get very hot. Small strawberries can go on the tarts whole, larger ones need to be cut in half. Lay the strawberries on a sheet of baking parchment and glaze them with the jam. Doing this before you put them on the tarts allows any excess glaze to run off rather than dripping on the curd. Using a small knife, place the glazed strawberries on top of the tartlets.

Choux Clouds

Choux pastry filled with cream has been engrained in my memory ever since my first school exchange to France. At the tender age of 13, we thought it was *très chic* to step into the local café and order *un choux et un coca*. I'm not so sure I would wash my choux buns down with Coca-Cola these days, but a nice cup of coffee – that would be highly desirable.

I'm on cloud nine with choux pastry – hence choux clouds. They are not quite as round as profiteroles, nor as straight as éclairs. In this recipe, the choux pastry is sprinkled with buttery crumble, which adds sweetness and extra flavour. I think they are best kept simple, with a filling of whipped double cream, either plain or flavoured with a liqueur such as Grand Marnier or Malibu.

Makes 16–20

For the choux pastry:

100ml water
100ml milk
50g salted butter, diced
¼ tsp caster sugar
100g plain flour, sifted
2 medium eggs, beaten

For the crumble topping:

½ quantity of Streusel
 (see page 208), chilled

For the filling:

400ml double cream
1 tbsp icing sugar,
 plus extra for dusting
50ml liqueur (optional)
some fresh berries,
 to serve (optional)

Heat the oven to 200°C/Gas Mark 6. Line a baking tray with baking parchment.

Put the water, milk, butter and sugar in a small, heavy-based pan and bring to the boil. Add the sifted flour, reduce the heat to medium and cook for a few minutes, stirring constantly with a wooden spoon, until the mixture starts to firm up and come together into a single mass. You will also notice a white film forming on the base of the pan.

Transfer the mixture to a bowl and leave to cool for a few minutes, stirring occasionally to release trapped heat. Either with a wooden spoon or with the paddle attachment if you are using a freestanding electric mixer, gradually beat in the eggs. Do this slowly, a tablespoon at a time, until very smooth, before adding more egg.

Transfer the mixture to a piping bag fitted with a 1cm plain nozzle and pipe small cloud shapes on to the lined baking tray – basically 2 or 3 interlocking blobs of slightly varying size. Be a little playful and let them billow as clouds do. Pipe the shapes at least 3cm apart, as they will expand during baking.

To add extra 'cloud effect' and more flavour, sprinkle each cloud with crumble, placing some larger pieces of crumble in the middle to enhance the effect. Bake for about 20 minutes, until the choux pastry is golden and the crumble cooked. Remove from the oven and leave to cool.

To fill the buns, slice each cloud open along one side, using a small serrated knife, so that it opens like a clam shell. Put the cream and icing sugar in a bowl and whip to soft peaks, then fold in any liqueur. Fill a piping bag fitted with a 1cm plain nozzle with the cream and pipe small blobs into the clouds. Close the tops and dust with a little icing sugar. Serve as they are, or with some fresh berries on the side.

Lemon and Currant Puffs

The melt-in-the-mouth quality of these mini baked cheesecakes makes them quite irresistible. Best of all, they are very easy to prepare, especially if you have some puff pastry in your freezer. A great way to speed up regular baking of these is to roll out a large batch of puff pastry, cut it into discs and freeze them, separated with baking parchment. You can then just remove 12 from the freezer and within minutes they will be thawed enough to line the tins, enabling you to cook them in less than 30 minutes.

They are wonderful served for afternoon tea, and go particularly well with a cup of Earl Grey. Once you've tasted these, you may want to experiment with other flavours. Try lime or orange zest instead or lemon, or soak raisins in rum and pair them with a vanilla-flavoured cheese mix.

Makes 12

250g puff pastry
(see page 207, or use a
good-quality bought
puff pastry)

200g cream cheese

finely grated zest of
1 unwaxed lemon

3 tbsp caster sugar

1 medium egg

1 medium egg yolk

40g ground almonds

2 tbsp currants

1 tbsp icing sugar
(optional)

Roll the pastry out on a lightly floured surface to 1–2 mm thick, then cut out circles with a 7.5cm pastry cutter. Lightly butter a bun tin and line with the puff pastry discs. Chill them while you prepare the filling.

Heat the oven to 180°C/Gas Mark 4. Using a spatula, mix the cream cheese, lemon zest and caster sugar together, then mix in the egg and egg yolk. Finally add the ground almonds and the currants.

Spoon the mixture into the pastry cases and bake for 15–20 minutes, until the tarts are lightly domed and golden.

Remove from the oven and leave to cool. Serve plain or dust with the icing sugar.

Very Berry Tartlets

These little tartlets are an absolute triumph – mouth-wateringly delicious, amazingly versatile and not difficult to achieve. Sharp fruits contrast brilliantly with the sweetness of the frangipane and the pastry base. Besides summer berries, plums, apricots, cherries, gooseberries and rhubarb can all be used. Although you could also make this in a 25cm tart tin, I love baking small tarts. They are a perfect little treat, and can be assembled in advance, refrigerated and then baked at the last minute to serve warm, simply dusted with icing sugar.

If they are served cold, I prefer them glazed with apricot jam. The glossy look brings out the colours in the fruit and preserves them for up to two days as well.

Makes 24

1 quantity of Sweet Pastry
(see page 206)

½ quantity of Almond
Cream (see page 210)

300g mixed berries

30g icing sugar (optional)

100g apricot glaze
(or apricot jam, heated
and strained through
a sieve)

Grease two 12-hole 5cm mini-muffin tins with a little butter. Roll out the pastry on a lightly floured surface to 3mm thick and cut out circles with a 6.5cm pastry cutter. Use them to line the tins, carefully pressing the pastry right down into the base.

Spoon or pipe in the almond cream – you need only about 10g for each tartlet. It's best to flatten the mixture with the back of a wet teaspoon or simply a moistened thumb. Chill for about 30 minutes. Heat the oven to 180°C/Gas Mark 4.

Remove the pastry cases from the fridge and place the fruits on top – you can be rustic or fan them out in a very orderly fashion. Bake for about 25 minutes, until the frangipane is golden.

Remove from the oven and leave to cool. After about 20 minutes, you should be able to ease the tartlets out of their tins.

Dust them very lightly with icing sugar and serve – they are at their best while still slightly warm. Or, if you are serving them cold, put the glaze or strained jam in a small saucepan and bring to boiling point, then remove from the heat – be careful, as it can get very hot. Brush the glaze carefully over the tarts with a pastry brush.

Monster Cookies

Sometimes there is a difference between professional and domestic kitchen equipment, particularly when it comes to ovens. All ovens have their own peculiarities. The best ones bake evenly all over and maintain the correct temperature. You can't always rely on this, though, so it's wise to use an oven thermometer to make sure that the temperature is the same as the one indicated. Gas ovens seem to produce a drier heat, which is great for scones; electric fan ovens are superb for multiple baking trays, as you might use when baking these cookies.

This recipe should produce moist, crumbly cookies. With a cooking time of only 8–10 minutes, it does very much come down to your knowledge of your oven to time it just right.

**Makes 8 large
or 16 mini cookies**

125g salted butter, softened

150g light soft brown sugar

1 medium egg

½ tsp vanilla extract

225g plain flour

1 tsp bicarbonate of soda

25g cocoa powder

100g white chocolate,
   chopped

40g walnuts, broken

Using an electric mixer, briefly beat the butter and sugar together in a bowl, being careful not to over-mix. Beat in the egg and vanilla extract.

Sift the flour, bicarbonate of soda and cocoa powder into a separate bowl or on to a sheet of baking parchment. Gradually work the dry ingredients into the butter mix, then add the white chocolate pieces and walnuts and combine well. Wrap the cookie dough in cling film and chill for 30 minutes.

Heat the oven to 180°C/Gas Mark 4. Divide the cookie dough into 8 large or 16 mini monster cookies, Roll them into balls, then squash them flat so they are 10–15mm thick. Place them about 2cm apart on a baking sheet lined with baking parchment and bake for 8–10 minutes. The cookies taste best if they are only just cooked – if the bases are a bit hard the first time round, either reduce the cooking time next time or see if you get a better result by putting them on a higher rack in the oven.

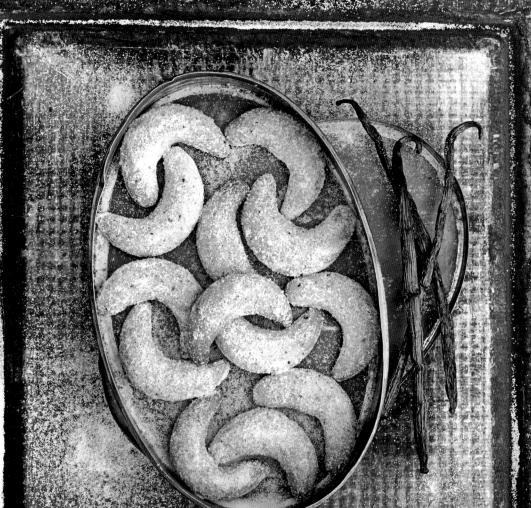

Kipferl Cookies

These typically Austrian cookies have spread to the far reaches of the former Habsburg Empire and are popular throughout southern Germany and in Hungary. Legend has it that the crescent shape is derived from the Turkish half moon. These days, Kipferl are a staple Christmas treat in Germany but can also be found throughout the year.

It is in this tradition that we bake them all year round at Konditor & Cook – or perhaps it's just to satisfy the human squirrels, who love the moreish taste of toasted hazelnuts and vanilla. After baking, the warm biscuits are rolled in vanilla sugar. It is quite handy to have a jar of vanilla sugar (see page 210) in your cupboard for this and other recipes. Otherwise, just add a small pinch of fresh vanilla seeds to a cup of caster sugar and mix well.

Makes 48

50g ground hazelnuts

60g caster sugar

1 egg yolk

½ tsp vanilla extract

125g salted butter, cut into
    sugar-cube-sized pieces

200g plain flour

100g vanilla sugar
    (see page 210)

Heat the oven to 180°C/Gas Mark 4. Spread out the ground hazelnuts on a baking sheet lined with baking parchment and toast them in the oven for 5–7 minutes, until golden brown. Remove from the oven and leave to cool.

In a mixing bowl, blend the caster sugar with the egg yolk and vanilla extract, using a wooden spoon. Add the cubed butter and mix until the pieces have broken down a little. Add the flour and toasted hazelnuts, stir together, then knead to a smooth dough with your hands.

Divide the dough into 3 pieces and roll each one into a sausage 16–20cm long. Cover with cling film and chill for 30 minutes.

Remove the dough from the fridge and cut each length into 16 pieces (half, then quarters, then eighths and so on). Roll each piece into a ball, then, using the palms of your hands, shape it into a small, tapered crescent moon. Don't make the ends too pointy or they will burn.

Place the Kipferl 1cm apart on a baking tray lined with baking parchment. Bake for about 12 minutes, until pale golden brown.

Remove from the oven and leave to cool for a minute or so, then push all the cookies towards the centre of the tray and sprinkle with the vanilla sugar. It's best to cover them completely. Leave to cool.

When the cookies are completely cold, lift them out of the vanilla sugar. They will keep in an airtight container for up to 2 months.

Mini Lemon Meringue Pies

These mini lemon meringues are a little labour of love and will disappear faster than you can make them. To give them that wonderful, toasted, two-tone finish, you will need a blowtorch – easily available from a DIY store.

Makes 24

1 quantity of **Sweet Pastry** (see page 206)

1 quantity of **Lemon Curd** (see page 214)

2 medium egg whites

a pinch of salt

a few drops of lemon juice

120g caster sugar

Grease two 12-hole 5cm mini-muffin tins with a little butter. Roll out the pastry on a lightly floured surface to 3mm thick and cut out circles with a 6.5cm fluted pastry cutter. Use them to line the tins, carefully pressing the pastry right down into the base. Chill for 30 minutes. Heat the oven to 180°C/Gas Mark 4.

Line each tartlet case with foil and fill with beans or rice to bake blind. Bake for 15 minutes, then remove from the oven, lift off the foil and beans or rice and return to the oven for about 5 minutes, until golden. Remove from the oven and leave to cool.

Pipe or spoon a heaped teaspoon of lemon curd into each tartlet.

To make the meringue, put the egg whites in a large, clean mixing bowl, add the salt and lemon juice and start beating with an electric mixer. Once bubbles begin to form, begin to add the sugar a tablespoonful at a time and beat until you have a stiff but silky-looking meringue.

Using a piping bag fitted with a 5mm plain nozzle, pipe circles of small peaks on each tartlet. Place in the oven with both the fan and grill switched on and leave for a few minutes, until browned – or use a blowtorch to caramelise the meringue evenly all over and give a defined two-tone effect.

Pecorino Biscuits

Baking is not all about sugar, so I thought these biscuits, made from an Italian sheep's milk cheese, would be a good addition to this book. They make a great edible gift. Next time you are invited to a dinner party, take a nice bottle of red and a small bowl filled with these biscuits – I'm sure you will be invited again!

We usually bake these around Christmas time, as they make very tasty blotting paper, and you can also use them as the base for savoury canapés. The biscuits are cut from a log of dough. You can freeze this and cut the biscuits whenever you need then – just transfer the dough to the fridge for a couple of hours before slicing.

Makes about 60

2 tsp finely chopped
   rosemary

½ tsp finely chopped
   oregano

300g plain flour, sifted

150g pecorino sardo cheese
   (or Parmesan cheese),
   finely grated

225g salted butter, chilled
   and cut into cubes

¼ tsp salt

Set aside half the rosemary. Place the rest in a bowl with all the other ingredients and work into a dough. You can do this with your hands or in a freestanding electric mixer fitted with the paddle attachment.

Divide the dough into 3 and roll each piece into a log about 3cm in diameter. Loosely sprinkle the reserved rosemary over the work surface and roll the logs in it to coat. Cover with cling film and chill for 1 hour. Heat the oven to 180°C/Gas Mark 4.

Remove the dough from the fridge and cut each log into slices 8–10mm thick.

Arrange 1cm apart on lightly buttered baking sheets and bake in the top half of the oven for about 10 minutes, until starting to colour lightly around the edges. Remove from the oven and leave to cool.

Variations: The logs can be rolled in a variety of seeds, such as fennel or poppy seeds, before being chilled.

You could also try shaping the logs to give different shaped biscuits – triangular and square biscuits are particularly striking.

To make square biscuits, roll the dough into a log and chill, as above, then use a small paring knife to cut the dough into an oblong block before slicing into square biscuits.

For triangles, roll the dough into a log, wrap it in cling film and then mould into a triangular block before rolling in seeds or herbs and chilling then slicing as above.

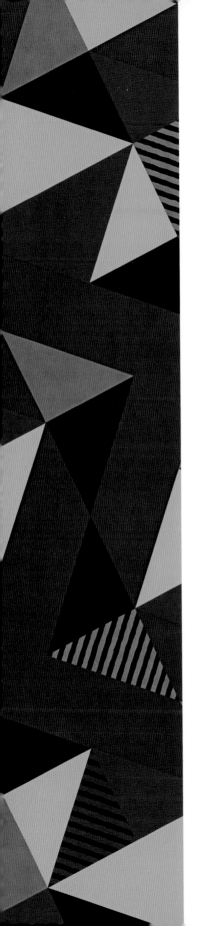

Brownies
and Slices

Chocolate Chip Brownies

This recipe is not for the fainthearted. It's rich and buttery and oozes with two types of chocolate. I remember when I first came to the UK, in the early 1980s, and baked at Justin de Blank's in Walton Street, London, the chocolate walnut brownies were made in a deep tray and had a cakey texture – nothing like modern brownies. Chocolate and nuts are a winning combination but today's brownies should be rich and slightly gooey, with a very chocolatey depth of flavour.

Our recipe contains more than 25 per cent chocolate, and the fact that we bake the equivalent of 3,000 chocolate bars every week should suffice as proof that this recipe is a hit. Timing is crucial to the success of a brownie: a few minutes too long in the oven will make them rise and give them a spongy texture. It's worth remembering that they continue to cook for a little while after being removed from the oven. Catch them earlier rather than late!

With a bit of practice you will be able to create freshly baked brownies in less than 30 minutes. They are best eaten fresh, and delicious served with ice cream or a dollop of thick double cream.

Makes 8 large,
16 medium or
32 cocktail-sized brownies

3 medium eggs

275g caster sugar

175g salted butter

200g dark chocolate (54–60 per cent cocoa solids), chopped into small pieces

100g dark chocolate (70 per cent cocoa solids), chopped into coffee-bean-sized pieces

175g plain flour

Heat the oven to 180°C/Gas Mark 4. Line a 20cm x 34cm baking tray with baking parchment.

Break the eggs into a mixing bowl, add the sugar and give a few whisks with a hand whisk or electric beater, then set aside. This helps the sugar start to dissolve.

Put the butter in a pan and leave over a medium heat until it has completely melted and small bubbles are just beginning to rise to the surface; be careful not to let it boil. Turn off the heat, then add all the 54–60 per cent chocolate and a third of the 70 per cent chocolate. Stir until melted.

Whisk the eggs a little more until they start to get paler, then whisk in the chocolate mix to make a smooth paste. Sift in the flour and stir gently with a spatula until completely combined. Finally stir in the remaining pieces of chocolate.

Pour the mixture into the lined tray and level with a spatula or palette knife. Bake for 18–20 minutes, until the brownies have reached the stage where the edges are starting to rise and crack slightly and the centre is soft to the touch but not liquid. Remember they do cook on even after they come out of the oven. Remove from the oven and leave to cool in the tray.

Cut into 8 large squares, 16 medium triangles or fingers, or 32 mini brownies. They should have a soft centre and fudgy appearance when cooled. If they are too spongy, reduce the baking time by a minute or two on your next attempt.

Apple Flapjacks with Pumpkin Seeds

This quick and easy recipe makes a fantastic treat for pesky Halloween trick-or-treaters, and is a great addition to a lunchbox at any time. Every year around Halloween, our shop in Borough Market helps to celebrate the market's Apple Festival. These apple flapjacks, with their wonderful chewy texture combined with the healthy bite of pumpkin seeds, are one of the recipes with which we celebrate.

Makes 12

1 large Bramley apple
  (about 200g)

¼ tsp ground cloves

200g unsalted butter

100g golden syrup

50g honey

90g light soft
  brown sugar

250g jumbo oats

125g porridge oats

3 tbsp pumpkin seeds

Heat the oven to 180°C/Gas Mark 4. Line a 20cm x 34cm baking tray with baking parchment.

Peel and core the apple, cut it into small cubes (about 8mm) and sprinkle with the ground cloves.

Put the butter, syrup, honey and sugar into a large pan and slowly bring to boiling point. Once it starts to bubble, simmer on a low heat for 30 seconds. Remove from the heat and add the oats and apple. Stir all the ingredients together with a spatula but be careful not to over-mix, as this will lead to a tougher texture.

Spread the mixture out in the lined baking tray and press flat with the back of a spoon. Sprinkle the pumpkin seeds on top.

Bake for 25–30 minutes, until golden brown. Remove from the oven and leave to cool. Chill for 1 hour before cutting into 12 squares or bars or, as we did in the picture shown opposite, into rounds using a straight-sided 5cm cutter. Believe you me, the leftover trimmings are just as delicious.

Tarta de Santiago

This recipe stems from a collaboration with Brindisa, a London-based Spanish food importer. Its founder, Monika Linton, and I share a common history because we have both worked at Justin de Blank. In 1998 Konditor & Cook became the first of a new family of food businesses that were on course to breathe new life into the almost-defunct Borough Market in south London. Brindisa soon followed, with its lock-up market stall and legendary chorizo and ciabatta rolls.

Membrillo, the Spanish quince paste, was one of the lesser-known ingredients in Brindisa's range. Besides being delicious with Manchego cheese, it is a key ingredient for this sort of posh Iberian Bakewell slice.

Tarta de Santiago makes a great accompaniment to tea and coffee but, since it is not overly sweet, it is also very nice paired with a glass of medium-dry wine or dessert wine.

Makes 8 large, 16 medium or 32 bite-sized pieces

For the pastry base:

40g caster sugar

1 tsp ground cinnamon

1 medium egg yolk

100g salted butter, cut into cubes

150g plain flour

For the filling:

200g quince paste

50g ground almonds

For the topping:

150g salted butter

100g caster sugar

grated zest of ½ unwaxed lemon

½ tsp ground cinnamon

150g ground almonds

150ml sweet sherry

3 medium eggs

First make the pastry base. Mix the sugar and cinnamon with the egg yolk, then add the cubed butter, followed by the flour. Briefly work into a dough with your hands, then cover and chill for 30 minutes.

Remove the dough from the fridge, knead it briefly, then roll out on a lightly floured surface to 2–3mm thick. Use to line a 20cm x 34cm baking tray. Chill the pastry while you prepare the filling.

Heat the oven to 180°C/Gas Mark 4. Place the quince paste in a shallow bowl, add the ground almonds and about 2 tablespoons of water and squash and blend them together with a fork (you could also do this in a food processor).

To make the topping, melt the butter in a pan over a low heat. Put all the remaining topping ingredients in a bowl and combine with a whisk. Add the melted butter and mix to what might seem a surprisingly runny paste.

Remove the pastry case from the fridge and spread the quince filling over the base, then pour the almond topping on top.

Place on a lower rack of the oven and bake for 35–40 minutes, until evenly browned and slightly springy on top. Remove from the oven and leave to cool.

Cut into 8 large squares, 16 medium triangles or fingers, or 32 mini squares.

Curly Whirly Brownies

The dark chocolate and vanilla Curly Whirly Cake (see page 14) is our most popular cake and, as befits something so popular, there are some spin offs. Our brownies are great ambassadors for our enduring quality and honest baking. It seemed natural, therefore, to create a Curly Whirly Brownie. The question was, how to get the vanilla frosting into it?

The frosting for the Curly Whirly Cake is made with icing sugar, cream cheese and vanilla. It just needed one extra ingredient to turn it into something that holds it together and bakes – egg, just as in a baked cheesecake.

Flavourwise, it was a match made in heaven. The Curly Whirly Brownie's cheese topping has a slightly cooling effect on the tongue, making it a nice brownie to enjoy even on a hot summer's day. For this recipe I recommend using a vanilla pod rather than vanilla extract. I find the seeds have a lot more character and are far more tantalising on the taste buds than the 'flat' extracts.

Makes 8 large, 16 medium or 32 cocktail-sized brownies

3 medium eggs

275g caster sugar

175g salted butter

200g dark chocolate (54–60 per cent cocoa solids), chopped into small pieces

100g dark chocolate (70 per cent cocoa solids), chopped into coffee-bean-sized pieces

175g plain flour

For the cheesecake topping:

200g cream cheese

75g icing sugar, sifted

seeds from ¼ vanilla pod

1 medium egg yolk

Heat the oven to 180°C/Gas Mark 4. Line a 20cm x 34cm baking tray with baking parchment.

Break the eggs into a mixing bowl, add the sugar and give a few whisks with a hand whisk or electric beater, then set aside. This helps the sugar start to dissolve.

Put the butter in a pan and leave over a medium heat until it has completely melted and small bubbles are just beginning to rise to the surface; be careful not to let it boil. Turn off the heat, then add the 54–60 per cent chocolate and a third of the 70 per cent chocolate. Stir until melted.

Whisk the eggs and sugar a little more until they turn paler, then add the chocolate mixture and mix to a smooth paste. Sift in the flour and stir with a wooden spoon until completely combined. Finally stir in the remaining pieces of chocolate. Pour the mixture into the lined tray and level with a spatula or palette knife.

To make the cheesecake topping, beat the cream cheese with the icing sugar and vanilla until smooth, then mix in the egg yolk.

Continued...

Transfer the mixture to a piping bag fitted with a 1cm nozzle and pipe it on to the brownie mix in parallel lines about 3cm apart. Drag a fork or knife through the cream cheese and the immediate surface of the chocolate mix to feather it. You are trying to achieve a slight mixing of the two. You could stick to straight lines or pipe swirls of the cream cheese mix on the surface. In the absence of a piping bag you could simply put small spoonfuls of the mixture on top, then drag a skewer or fork through it.

Bake for 22–25 minutes in the top half of the oven. My oven has 4 runners and I generally bake on the second one up; for these brownies, however, I always use the third one up. This should guarantee that the cheesecake topping develops some colour without overcooking the brownies in the process. Leave to cool in the baking tray. The brownies should have a soft centre and fudgy appearance when cooled. If they are too spongy, reduce the baking time by a minute or two on your next attempt.

Cut into 8 large squares, 16 medium triangles or fingers, or 32 mini brownies.

Hot Cross Blondies

Our brownies have developed a bit of a cult following. Throughout the year we offer at least four different varieties, as well as seasonal specials. For Easter, we created a chocolate blondie substituting white chocolate for dark and drawing on the 'botanicals' featured in hot cross buns – namely mixed spice, orange peel, currants and almonds.

The blondies are topped with an almond lattice. If you want your cross to go perfectly through the middle of each blondie, you have to decide in advance how you want to cut them. It's also just as good to add the almond lattice in a freestyle pattern (or omit it altogether). And you certainly don't need Easter as a reason to bake these. Served slightly warm with a scoop of vanilla ice cream, they make a delicious dessert all year round.

Makes 8 large blondies

1 unwaxed orange

50g mixed candied peel

75g currants

250g caster sugar

¼ tsp vanilla extract

2 medium eggs

1 medium egg yolk

150g salted butter

125g white chocolate,
  chopped

175g plain flour

¼ tsp baking powder

½ tsp ground mixed spice

¼ tsp ground cardamom

¼ tsp ground nutmeg

For the almond lattice:

40g ground almonds

40g icing sugar

1 medium egg white,
  lightly beaten
  with a fork

Heat the oven to 180°C/Gas Mark 4. Line a 20cm x 34cm baking tray with baking parchment.

Grate the zest of the orange and squeeze the juice of half of it. Place the mixed peel and currants in a bowl, pour over the orange juice and leave to soak. Put the orange zest in a mixing bowl together with the sugar, vanilla extract, eggs and egg yolk. Give a few whisks with a hand whisk or electric beater, then set aside. This helps the sugar start to dissolve.

Put the butter in a pan and leave over a medium heat until it has completely melted and small bubbles are just beginning to rise to the surface; be careful not to let it boil. Turn off the heat, then add about two-thirds of the white chocolate and stir until melted.

Sift the flour into a bowl with the baking powder and add the spices. Whisk the eggs a little more until they start to get paler, then whisk in the chocolate mix to a make a smooth paste. Using an electric mixer on slow speed or a spatula, mix in the flour and spices, being careful not to over-mix.

Drain the excess juice from the currants and candied peel. Add the currants and peel to the mixture with the remaining white chocolate and mix evenly. Pour the mixture into the lined tray and level with a spatula or palette knife.

Continued...

To make the almond lattice, put the ground almonds in a bowl, sift in the icing sugar and add enough egg white to give a soft paste. It should be the correct consistency for piping in thin lines over the blondies, but be careful not to make it too runny.

Put the almond paste in a piping bag fitted with a 5mm nozzle and pipe it over the blondie mixture. If you want your crosses to be perfectly spaced through the middle of each blondie, you must virtually divide the blondies in the tray first. Marking the top with a knife is difficult, as the mix is too runny. You might want to rely on a rough estimate, or you could place a ruler or marked strips of paper down the sides of the tray indicating where to pipe. Of course, you could also pipe a random lattice pattern.

Bake for 22–25 minutes, then remove from the oven and leave to cool in the tray. The blondies should have a soft centre and fudgy appearance when cooled. If they are too spongy, reduce the baking time slightly on your next attempt. Cut into 8 large squares, or try cutting them into rounds to look like hot cross buns. These blondies are very moreish and any leftover trimmings will disappear in no time.

Whisky and Fig Brownies

This is definitely a brownie for grown-ups. Its boozy nature makes it an ideal dessert, especially in winter. We use Doves Farm gluten-free flour and egg whites rather than whole eggs, to give the mixture more stability. Of course, you can also make this with regular flour, in which case you can replace the egg whites with 3 medium whole eggs. Other brownie recipes can be adapted to gluten-free flour in this way, but bear in mind they might take a little longer to bake.

Makes 8 large, 16 medium or 32 cocktail-sized brownies

150g dried or semi-dried figs, plus a few extra to serve

40ml whisky

4 medium egg whites

275g caster sugar

175g salted butter

200g dark chocolate (54 per cent cocoa solids), chopped into small pieces

175g gluten-free flour, such as Doves Farm

75g white chocolate, chopped into coffee-bean-sized pieces

1 tbsp cocoa powder

thick double cream, to serve

Remove the hard stem from the figs, cut each fig into quarters, then place in a bowl and pour over the whisky. Leave to soak for at least 2 hours, preferably overnight.

Heat the oven to 180°C/Gas Mark 4. Line a 20cm x 34cm baking tray with baking parchment.

Put the egg whites in a mixing bowl, add the sugar and give a few whisks with a hand whisk or electric beater, then set aside. This helps the sugar start to dissolve.

Put the butter in a pan and leave over a medium heat until it has completely melted and small bubbles are just beginning to rise to the surface; be careful not to let it boil. Turn off the heat, then add the dark chocolate and stir until melted.

Whisk the egg whites and sugar for a couple of minutes more, then whisk in the chocolate mixture until smooth. Sift in the flour and stir gently with a spatula until completely combined. Finally, stir in the white chocolate and the figs, including any whisky that hasn't been absorbed.

Pour the mixture into the lined tray and level with a spatula or palette knife. Bake for about 25 minutes, until the sides have risen up a little and started to crack, then remove from the oven and leave to cool in the tray.

Cut into slender fingers or 8 large squares, 16 medium triangles or 32 mini brownies, then dust with cocoa powder. Serve with cream and extra figs on the side.

Ninja Slice

London's baking scene has exploded over the last decade, which for commercial bakers means that marketing your product in the right way is important when trying to have the edge over increasing competition. One of our goals at Konditor & Cook is to provide customers with an everyday treat, and we achieve this not only with some good, honest baking but also by adding a healthy dose of humour to the mix. From an 'anti-depressant' Chocolate Biscuit Cake (see page 42) to the quite controversial fudgepacker brownie – a brownie packed with fudge – the name of a product can have as much to do with its success as can the recipe itself.

The Ninja Slice has all the appeal of a date and walnut slice but, while the latter name is reminiscent of grandmotherly, doily-stuffed tearooms, calling it a Ninja Slice gives it new powers and makes it very popular indeed – and the addition of banana gives your potassium levels a boost. Serve with a dollop of cream or, slightly warmed, with a big scoop of vanilla ice cream for a wintry pudding with a punchy flavour.

Makes 8 large, 16 medium or 32 mini slices

1 quantity of Butter Shortbread dough (see page 208)

125g salted butter, softened

150g dark muscovado sugar

3 medium eggs, lightly beaten

120g ground almonds

1 medium banana

120g dates, chopped into 3–4 pieces each

60g walnuts, chopped

60g flaked almonds

Heat the oven to 180°C/Gas Mark 4. Line a 20cm x 34cm baking tray with baking parchment.

Press the shortbread dough into the tray and level it with the back of a spoon or a rolling pin. Bake for 15 minutes until it is lightly coloured, then remove from the oven and leave to cool, but do not turn the oven off.

Using an electric mixer, beat the butter and muscovado sugar until the mixture begins to look paler and fluffy. Gradually beat in the eggs, alternating them with the ground almonds and scraping down the sides of the bowl with a spatula occasionally. After the last bit of egg, add the remainder of the ground almonds.

Peel the banana, mash it roughly with a fork and add it to the mixture, along with the dates, walnuts and flaked almonds. Stir in with a spatula or with the mixer on a slow speed.

Spread the mixture on to the shortbread base and level the top. Bake at 180°C/Gas Mark 4 for 25–30 minutes, until it is evenly browned and the top is slightly springy when lightly tapped with a finger.

Remove from the oven and leave to cool, then cut into 8 large squares, 16 medium triangles or 32 mini squares.

Bakewell Slab

This easy recipe is a three-layer affair of shortbread base, jam filling and almond frangipane topping. Not to be confused with the Bakewell pudding, Bakewell tarts or slices have been enduringly popular since the mid-nineteenth century. We fill ours with a layer of lovely raspberry jam. In fact, it's a particularly great one, made by Sky and Kai of England Preserves. Sky and Kai met at Konditor & Cook while working in our Borough Market shop. They went on to set up their own successful jam and preserve business, selling to all the best hotels and retailers in town.

I urge you to try this recipe, as it is so very popular with young and old alike. By varying the jam, you can give it your own spin. Apricot jam works very well and so does blackberry. Get baking!

Makes 8 large, 16 medium or 32 mini slices

1 quantity of Butter Shortbread dough (see page 208)

150g salted butter, softened

150g caster sugar

3 medium eggs, lightly beaten

150g ground almonds

150g raspberry jam

30g flaked almonds

Heat the oven to 180°C/Gas Mark 4. Line a 20cm x 34cm baking tray with baking parchment.

Press the shortbread dough into the tray and level it with the back of a spoon or a rolling pin. Bake for 15 minutes, until starting to turn golden, then remove from the oven and leave to cool. Reduce the oven temperature to 165°C/Gas Mark 3.

To make the frangipane, beat the butter and sugar together with an electric mixer for about 2 minutes, until thoroughly combined. Gradually beat in the eggs, alternating them with the ground almonds.

Spread the shortbread base with the raspberry jam, then pour the frangipane mix on top and spread it out evenly. Sprinkle with the flaked almonds.

Bake for about 25 minutes, turning the tray around halfway through, if necessary, so that the slab colours evenly. To check whether it is done, tap the surface: if it springs back, it is cooked; if it leaves an indent or the top breaks, it needs a little longer. Remove from the oven and leave to cool.

Cut into 8 large squares or fingers, 16 medium triangles or 32 mini slices.

Boston Brownies

Everyone loves chocolate and rich, indulgent brownies are a failsafe choice. This is a hugely popular recipe, and very easy too. Serve the brownies as small treats, cut into slender fingers, or, for a quick dessert, warm them slightly and serve with lashings of cream or a scoop of vanilla ice cream.

This recipe includes cranberries, and the name was inspired by a trip to Massachusetts, where I saw the cranberry bogs and sampled the fruit in muffins for my breakfast. I loved the kick and sharpness of these little red wonders, and thought they would make a great combination with dark chocolate. In this, the Boston brownie is like black forest gâteau, where the sharpness of the cherries cuts through the richness of the chocolate sponge and cream.

Makes 8 large, 16 medium or 32 cocktail-sized brownies

3 medium eggs

275g caster sugar

175g salted butter

200g dark chocolate (54–60 per cent cocoa solids), chopped into small pieces

175g plain flour

1 tbsp cocoa powder

175g fresh cranberries (or thawed frozen cranberries)

15g icing sugar (optional)

Heat the oven to 180°C/Gas Mark 4. Line a 20cm x 34cm baking tray with baking parchment.

Break the eggs into a mixing bowl, add the sugar and give a few whisks with a hand whisk or electric beater, then set aside. This helps the sugar start to dissolve.

Put the butter in a pan and leave over a medium heat until it has completely melted and small bubbles are just beginning to rise to the surface; be careful not to let it boil. Turn off the heat, then add the chocolate and stir until melted.

Whisk the eggs and sugar until they are a little paler, then add the chocolate mixture and mix to a smooth paste. Sift in the flour and cocoa powder and stir gently with a spatula until completely combined. Finally stir the cranberries briefly into the mix.

Pour the mixture into the lined tray and level the top with a spatula or palette knife. Bake for about 30 minutes, then remove from the oven and leave to cool in the tray. The brownies should have a soft centre and fudgy appearance when cooled. If they are too spongy, reduce the baking time slightly on your next attempt.

Cut into 8 large squares, 16 medium triangles or fingers, or 32 mini brownies. Dust lightly with the icing sugar before serving, if liked.

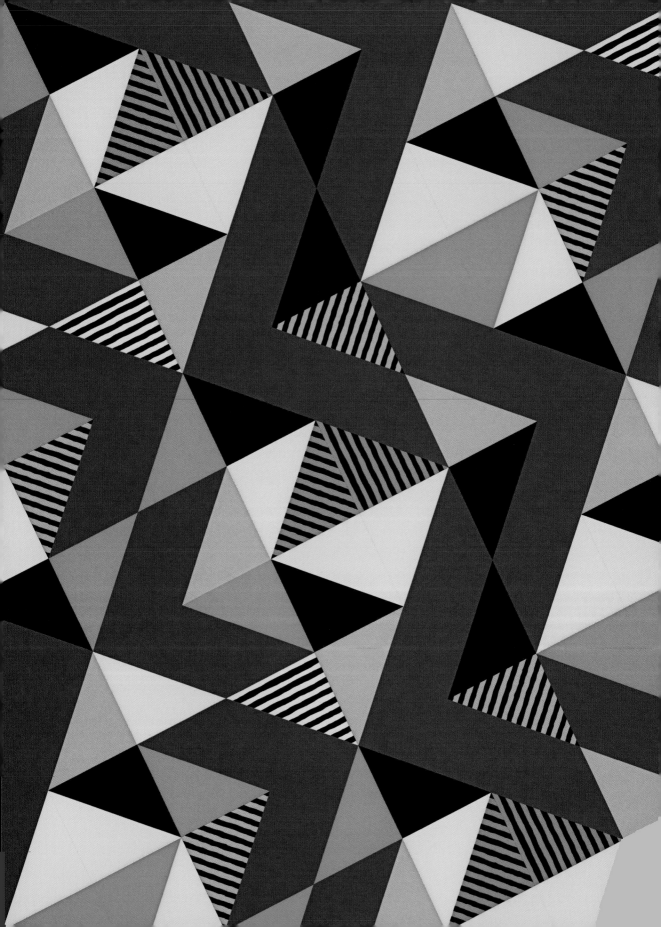

Muffins, Cupcakes and Buns

Black Velvet Cupcakes with Irish Cream Frosting

Of all the national holidays, St Patrick's Day stands out as the liveliest. Is this because the Irish like a good party, or has it more to do with the fact that it falls on 17 March, a day still steeped in winter darkness that calls for some seasonal cheer?

At Konditor & Cook, St Patrick's Day has to include these Black Velvet Cupcakes, named after the cocktail featuring Guinness and champagne but actually containing another of Ireland's famous tipples, Bailey's Irish Cream. The stout gives the cakes a malty flavour, while the Irish Cream frosting adds some fingerlickingly gorgeous sweetness.

Makes 12

125ml milk

100g dark chocolate (54 per cent cocoa solids), chopped

325g light soft brown sugar

125g salted butter, softened

225g plain flour

1 tbsp cocoa powder

1 tsp bicarbonate of soda

1 tsp baking powder

2 medium eggs, lightly beaten

200ml Guinness (or other stout)

To decorate:

½ quantity of Cream Cheese Frosting (see page 211), flavoured with the seeds of ½ vanilla pod and about 25ml Bailey's Irish Cream liqueur

a little cocoa powder or 50g dark chocolate

Heat the oven to 180°C/Gas Mark 4. Line a muffin tin with 12 paper cupcake cases.

Put the milk, chocolate and half the sugar in a saucepan. Bring to the boil over a low heat, stirring occasionally. Remove from the heat.

Using an electric mixer, beat the butter with the remaining sugar until light and fluffy. Sift the flour, cocoa powder, bicarbonate of soda and baking powder into a separate bowl. Turn the mixer down to a low speed and beat the eggs into the butter mixture in about 4 stages, alternating each addition with a couple of tablespoons of the flour mix. When all the egg has been added, mix in the remaining flour.

Add the stout, with the mixer still on a low speed, and finally pour in the still-warm chocolate mix. Mix slowly for a couple of minutes, until the mixture is smooth and runny.

Using a ladle or a jug, pour the mixture into the paper cases. Bake for about 25 minutes, until a skewer inserted in the centre comes out clean. Remove from the oven and leave to cool completely.

Spoon the frosting on to the cupcakes and shape into a shallow dome using a small palette knife, or pipe it on using a piping bag fitted with a 1cm nozzle. Dust with a little cocoa powder, if you like (you could cut out a shamrock template).

Alternatively, for the real thing, decorate the top of each cake with a chocolate shamrock or harp. If you have confident piping skills, put the melted chocolate in a parchment piping bag (see page 216) and pipe it straight on top of each cake. Otherwise draw templates on a piece of paper, place a piece of baking parchment over it and follow the templates with your piping. Refrigerate until set, then lift off and transfer to the cakes.

Blueberry Muesli Muffins

This healthy recipe is very easy to make. It is a dairy-free muffin that has become a staple of our breakfast range and is a good way to stave off those mid-morning hunger pangs. Make a large batch and freeze some, if you wish. To defrost, remove them from the freezer the night before and leave them in the fridge overnight (or at room temperature for about 4 hours). Warm them for about 5 minutes in an oven preheated to 150°C/Gas Mark 2 for that 'just-baked' feel.

Makes 10

2 medium bananas

150g golden caster sugar

200g blueberries
(fresh or frozen – if
using frozen berries
defrost partially at least
before using)

2 medium eggs

150g dessert apple, grated
coarsely, skin on

150g carrot, finely grated

75–100ml soya milk

100g good-quality bought
muesli mix (or use
porridge oats), plus
extra for sprinkling

300g self-raising flour

1 tsp baking powder

Heat the oven to 180°C/Gas Mark 4. Line a muffin tin with 10 paper muffin cases (for a more even bake, leave the 2 central holes clear).

Peel the bananas and mash them in a large bowl with a fork. Set aside 2 tablespoons of the sugar and 50g of the blueberries, then add all the rest of the ingredients to the bananas. Blend together with a whisk or spatula, being careful not to overmix.

Divide the mixture between the muffin cases. Sprinkle with the reserved sugar and blueberries, and scatter over a little extra muesli or a few more oat flakes.

Bake for about 25 minutes, until well risen and golden. If you don't eat them immediately, these muffins should be stored in the fridge, where they will keep for 3 days.

Dorset Apple Cakes

If you had to define the difference between English and German tastes, this cupcake would provide a good example. British taste buds favour sweet/sharp flavours, like chutneys or, in this case, apples paired with lemon. German bakers would reach for the spice jar instead, partnering apples with cinnamon or cloves. I rather like these spongy, moist cakes. Their sharp, lemony flavour, combined with toasted almonds and cream, makes them a lovely addition to afternoon tea.

Makes 12

4 medium dessert apples, such as Braeburn or Discovery

juice and grated zest of 1 unwaxed lemon

250g salted butter, softened

250g caster sugar

250g self-raising flour

½ tsp baking powder

4 medium eggs, lightly beaten

25g ground almonds

2 tbsp light soft brown sugar (or caster sugar)

25g flaked almonds

350ml double cream

1 tbsp icing sugar (optional)

Heat the oven to 180°C/Gas Mark 4. Line a muffin tin with 12 paper cupcake cases, or make your own rustic cases (see page 215).

Peel and core the apples, cut them into quarters, then cut each quarter into 3 long segments. Put the apple pieces in a bowl and toss with the lemon juice.

Using an electric mixer, beat the butter, caster sugar and lemon zest together for 2–3 minutes, until pale and fluffy.

Sift the flour and baking powder into a separate bowl. Beat about a quarter of the eggs into the butter and sugar, then add the ground almonds and about a quarter of the flour. Repeat 3 times until they are all used up, finishing with flour.

Divide the mixture between the cupcake cases. Push 4 apple segments into each one, with the narrow side of each segment towards the centre. Sprinkle the cakes with the soft brown sugar.

Bake for 30–35 minutes, until the cakes are golden brown and risen and a toothpick inserted in the centre comes out clean. Remove from the oven and leave to cool for at least 30 minutes.

Spread the flaked almonds out on a baking tray and toast them in the dying heat of the oven for about 5 minutes, until golden. Keep an eye on them, as they can go from light to burned very quickly. Remove from the oven and leave to cool.

Before serving, whip the cream to soft peaks, just so it easily drops from a spoon. Place a dollop of cream on each cake. Sprinkle with the toasted almonds and add a light dusting of icing sugar, if you like.

Wheat-free Hazelnut Cupcakes with Hazelnut Buttercream

This is a really moist and nutty cupcake, with the added advantage of being a wheat- and gluten-free recipe. Increasingly, many cake-loving customers are in search of delicious 'free-from' recipes and this is one of a number we have developed over the years. Anyone who loves hazelnuts will find this recipe irresistible. Besides baking it as a cupcake at Konditor & Cook, we have also baked it in individual silicone moulds and covered it with chocolate. We finish these cupcakes with a vanilla frosting containing gianduja chocolate. You can buy this chocolate online but, to make things easier, here I have suggested a Nutella-based buttercream that is easy to whip up, so that all the ingredients are readily available from supermarkets.

Makes 10

200g ground hazelnuts

75g ground almonds

¾ tsp gluten-free baking powder

200g unsalted butter, softened

200g caster sugar

4 medium eggs, lightly beaten

For the hazelnut buttercream:

175g unsalted butter, softened

175g Nutella

90g full-fat cream cheese

175g icing sugar (some icing sugar contains wheat starch, so check the packet)

50g whole skinned hazelnuts, lightly toasted (or chocolate sprinkles)

Some ground hazelnuts are pre-toasted. Alternatively, heat the oven to 180°C/Gas Mark 4, spread the hazelnuts out on a baking tray lined with baking parchment and toast in the oven for 5–7 minutes, until light brown. Leave to cool, then mix with the almonds and baking powder.

Reduce the oven temperature to 165°C/Gas Mark 3. Line a muffin tin with 10 paper cupcake cases (for a more even bake, leave the 2 central holes clear).

Using an electric mixer, cream the butter and sugar together for 2–3 minutes, until light and fluffy. Gradually beat in the eggs, alternating them with a couple of tablespoons of the ground nuts and scraping down the side of the bowl regularly. Once all the egg has been added, fold in the rest of the nuts.

Divide the mixture between the cupcake cases and bake for about 25 minutes, until a skewer inserted in the centre comes out clean. These cupcakes do not rise as much as wheat-based ones. Remove from the oven and leave to cool completely.

To make the hazelnut buttercream, use an electric mixer to beat the butter, Nutella and cream cheese together till smooth. Reduce the speed, sift in the icing sugar and beat for a further minute or two, until light and fluffy.

Using a piping bag fitted with a 5cm nozzle, pipe a succession of small swirls and crescents on top of each cupcake to form a mound, then sprinkle with the hazelnuts (or chocolate sprinkles, if you prefer).

Apple Crumble Muffins

Making muffins is one of the best ways to get into baking. It requires very little equipment and the method is usually quite simple. It's something that can be enjoyed by children too. These muffins are one of Konditor & Cook's autumnal treats. The crumble topping combines honey and poppy seeds but if you can't get hold of poppy seeds, nibbed almonds would work well.

Makes 10

350g dessert apples, such as Braeburn or Discovery

juice and grated zest of 1 unwaxed lemon

200g caster sugar

1 medium egg

125ml single cream

275g self-raising flour

1 tsp baking powder

For the poppy seed honey crumble:

50g unsalted butter, cut into cubes

30g caster sugar

2 tsp honey

100g plain flour

1 tbsp poppy seeds

First prepare the crumble. In a small bowl, mix the butter with the sugar and honey, then add the flour and rub together until the mixture looks like breadcrumbs. Add the poppy seeds and mix until everything starts to clump together. Refrigerate while making the muffin mix.

Heat the oven to 180°C/Gas Mark 4. Line a muffin tin with 10 homemade rustic muffin cases (see page 215) or use brown tulip cupcake cases (for a more even bake, leave the 2 central holes clear).

Core the apples but do not peel them. Cut them into 1cm cubes, mix with the lemon juice and zest and set aside.

Put the caster sugar, egg and cream into a bowl, whisk briefly, then stir in the apples with a spatula. Sift in the flour and baking powder and mix gently until just combined; do not over-mix.

Divide the mixture between the muffin cases and sprinkle evenly with the crumble. Bake for 25–30 minutes, until well-risen and golden.

Iced Prune Buns

My sister was engaged to the village baker and got me a summer job cleaning the baking trays and generally lending a hand at her fiancé's *Backstube*. This somewhat sealed my fate. Three months later my alarm clock rang at 3.30am and my life as a trainee baker started in earnest. I learned all about bread making but also baking with yeast in other forms: as a base for tarts, for voluminous plaits or individual buns.

Years later at Konditor & Cook, I was in search of a lighter alternative to croissants and brioches as a morning pastry when I remembered a plain, butter 'steamed' bun we used to make. I built on that and created the prune bun. It quickly became very popular. Indeed, one lady regularly introduced herself as Mrs Prune Bun. For years, she placed birthday cake orders for her children, Rufus and Araminta, under the name, Prune Bun. Her children must be quite grown up now and the bun has also evolved, since it now boasts the addition of lemon and cardamom.

Served with hot chocolate, these buns take me down memory lane on a journey to the flavours of the Orient.

Makes 12

1 quantity of Bun Dough (see page 209), with the grated zest of 1 unwaxed lemon and the crushed seeds of 4 cardamom pods added

12 dried or canned prunes, pitted

100g unsalted butter

For the icing:

150g icing sugar

juice of 1 lemon

a little candied lemon zest, made following the recipe for Candied Orange Zest on page 161 (optional)

Once the dough has risen and doubled in volume, divide it into 12 equal portions. Shape them into balls using the following method: place 2 pieces of dough on a very lightly floured work surface (don't use too much flour, as you need some traction). Cradle and cover each ball with one of your hands, keeping your thumbs flat on the surface and your fingertips turned inwards. Now start an outward circular motion. The hand movement starts to rotate the dough portions and begins to shape them into balls. The thumbs give them traction and within a few spins the dough balls start to develop a seam at the base and a smooth, silky skin on top.

When you have shaped all the balls, cover them with a tea towel and leave to relax for 10 minutes.

Turn the dough balls over and press them flat with your hands or a rolling pin (they should be about 8cm in diameter). Place a prune in the middle of each one, lift up the sides around the prune and seal by pinching the dough together.

Continued...

Cut the butter into 12 pieces and place them in the indents of a 12-hole muffin tray. Briefly warm the tray by placing it in a warm oven or by moving it around over a gas flame until the butter has just melted. The warmth will also help the buns to prove. Use a pastry brush to brush a little bit of butter up the sides of the holes, then place the buns, seam-side down, in the tray; when the buns are turned out after baking, the buttered side will be the top. Cover loosely with cling film and leave to rise until small domes appear just over the edge of each indent. Heat the oven to 180°C/Gas Mark 4.

Bake the buns for about 25 minutes, until they are light golden. The domes will spread over the edges, giving them a turban-like appearance. Remove from the oven and leave to cool in the tin for 30 minutes before turning them out.

To finish, sift the icing sugar into a bowl and stir in just enough lemon juice to make a thickish, spreadable icing. Turn the buns out of the tray, leaving them to wobble on their rounded sides. If you are a perfectionist, I recommend piping the icing on to the buns so that 'tears' of icing run down just so. Otherwise, spread it over the top of each bun with a spoon. Decorate with candied lemon zest, if liked.

Beasty Buns

These should really be called 'Beesting Buns'; the bastardisation of the name came from the fact that one customer could not pronounce it properly. And beasty they are, with their almond florentine topping and vanilla mascarpone filling. Their origin lies in the *Bienenstich*, a classic German tray bake or round cake. Traditionally it is filled with a vanilla custard that has been lightened by folding whipped meringue into it.

Most cake shops have succumbed to commercial pressure and now use an instant cold cream to fill this scrumptious cake. Here, vanilla mascarpone frosting makes a delicious alternative, or you could fill them with 500ml whipped double cream, like a Devonshire split. Finely sliced walnuts make a gourmet alternative to flaked almonds, but it requires a bit of time to slice them by hand. These buns are delicious with tea or coffee or as a sweet for a picnic.

Makes 12

1 quantity of Bun Dough (see page 209)

1–1½ quantities of Mascarpone Frosting, flavoured with vanilla (see page 213)

For the florentine topping:

50g unsalted butter

50ml single cream

50g caster sugar

25g honey

100g flaked almonds

a pinch of ground cinnamon

¼ tsp vanilla extract

First make the florentine topping. Put the butter, cream, sugar and honey in a small saucepan and heat gently until the butter has melted. Bring to a simmer and cook for 10 minutes. If you have a sugar thermometer, check the temperature; it should be 106°C – known as the thread stage. If you don't have a thermometer, you can test it by letting a little of the mixture drop off a spoon into cold water to see if it forms a thread. It should not at this stage have turned to caramel. Remove from the heat and add the flaked almonds, cinnamon and vanilla extract.

Divide the risen bun dough into 12 portions. Shape them into balls using the following method: place 2 pieces of dough on a very lightly floured work surface (don't use too much flour, as you need some traction), then cradle and cover each ball with one of your hands, keeping your thumbs flat on the surface and your fingertips turned inwards. Now start an outward circular motion. The hand movement rotates the dough portions and shapes them into balls, while the thumbs give them traction. Within a few spins, the dough balls should start to develop a seam at the base and a smooth, silky skin on top.

When you have shaped all the balls, cover them with a tea towel and leave to relax for 10 minutes. Then press them flat with your hands or a rolling pin until they are about 8cm in diameter. Top the buns with the florentine mixture, leaving a border of roughly 1cm all round (otherwise the almonds will fall off as the buns rise).

Continued...

Grease a baking tray or line it with baking parchment. Place the buns on it, spaced well apart, and leave until they double in size. Ideally you would do this in a warm spot that is not too dry. If you have the luxury of a plate-warmer or airing cupboard, make use of it.

Heat the oven to 180°C/Gas Mark 4. Bake the buns on the middle shelf for about 25 minutes, until the dough is lightly browned and the almonds look toasted. Remove from the oven and leave to cool.

Split the buns and spread with the mascarpone frosting, as if buttering bread for sandwiches. For total luxury, use the larger quantity of frosting and put it in a piping bag fitted with a 1cm plain nozzle. Pipe a ring of frosting around the perimeter of the bottom half of each bun, then sandwich with the top halves.

Carrot and Walnut Cupcakes

This is an easy recipe with a mouth-wateringly delicious result, rather like the famous passion cake. Dense and moist, it is so good that it's hard to believe there was once a time when people shunned the idea of using carrots in cakes. Someone clever had to come up with the name passion cake in order to get people to accept it – or so I've been told.

In Switzerland there is a traditional carrot cake known as *Rüeblitorte*, a light carrot sponge covered in jam and fondant icing and usually decorated with marzipan carrots.

As an alternative to cupcakes, you could also bake this mixture in two 20cm sandwich tins, then slice each cake in half horizontally and fill and top them with layers of the frosting.

Makes 12

1 unwaxed orange

400g carrots, finely grated

125g unsalted butter, softened

225g caster sugar

½ tsp vanilla extract

2 medium eggs, lightly beaten

50g walnuts, chopped

175g plain flour

1 tsp bicarbonate of soda

½ tsp ground mixed spice

¼ tsp salt

To decorate:

1 quantity of Mascarpone Frosting, flavoured with the seeds of ½ vanilla pod (see page 213)

75g caster sugar

Heat the oven to 180°C/Gas Mark 4. Line a muffin tin with 12 paper cupcake cases.

Remove 24 fine strips of zest from the orange with a zester, or use a vegetable peeler and then cut the zest into 1mm-wide pieces with a small knife. Set them aside for the topping. Grate the rest of the zest (you should have about a teaspoon). Mix the grated carrots with 2 tablespoons of juice from the orange.

Put the butter, sugar, grated orange zest and vanilla in a bowl and beat with an electric mixer until light and fluffy. Gradually beat in the eggs. Fold in the grated carrots and walnuts. Then sift in the flour, bicarbonate of soda, mixed spice and salt and fold them in.

Divide the mixture between the cupcake cases and bake for about 25 minutes, until the cupcakes are golden brown and a skewer inserted in the centre comes out clean. Remove from the oven and leave to cool completely.

Spoon the frosting on to the cupcakes and shape into a dome using a small palette knife. Alternatively you could pipe it on using a piping bag fitted with a 6mm nozzle.

Put the 75g caster sugar in a small saucepan, add 75ml water and bring to the boil, stirring to dissolve the sugar. Add the strips of orange zest to the boiling sugar syrup. Turn down the heat and simmer for 7 minutes. Be careful not to let it caramelise too much or it will burn spectacularly.

Remove from the heat and, using a fork, fish the strips of peel out of the syrup and place on a piece of baking parchment to cool. Use to decorate the top of the cupcakes. For a simpler decoration, you could also just grate some orange zest over the top of the frosted cupcakes, or finely chop some mixed peel and then sprinkle it over.

English Scones

Scones are a great way to get into baking. They are quick and easy to make, and you can really get stuck in and feel the dough. Home-made ones are decidedly superior to shop-bought versions.

Having extensively sampled cream teas in Devon, I have discovered that no two scones are ever alike. At Konditor & Cook we like our scones to rise nicely, even split slightly on the side so that you can just about pull them into a top and bottom half without using a knife. It is important that the dough is quite soft and that you barely knead it. You will notice that it likes to stick to your hands, but that is just what's required. Unfilled, baked scones can be frozen for up to 2 months.

Makes 12

400g self-raising flour

¾ tsp baking powder

60g caster sugar

80g salted butter, cut into small cubes

3 medium eggs

100ml milk

80g sultanas

To serve:

150g strawberry jam

150g clotted cream (or whipped double cream, if you cannot get clotted cream)

12–15 strawberries

2 tbsp icing sugar

Heat the oven to 220°C/Gas Mark 7 (scones like a hot, dry oven). Line a baking sheet with baking parchment.

Sift the flour and baking powder into a bowl and add the caster sugar. Mix well with a wooden spoon. Add the butter and rub it in with your fingertips until the mixture resembles fine crumbs.

Separate one of the eggs, putting the egg white into a jug and the yolk into a small bowl. Add a tablespoon of the milk to the egg yolk and whisk together with a fork. Set this egg wash aside for glazing the scones. Add the remaining eggs and the remaining milk to the egg white and whisk together.

Add the liquids to the dry ingredients and work them until they start coming together into a dough. At first it will be quite sticky, then turn lumpy. At this point, add the sultanas, working them lightly into the mix until it forms a smooth, soft dough.

On a lightly floured surface, roll or press out the dough to about 2.5cm thick. Cut into circles using a 6.5cm pastry cutter or a glass with a similar diameter. Place the scones 2cm apart on the lined baking sheet and, using a pastry brush, evenly glaze the tops with the egg wash. Bake in the top half of the oven for about 10 minutes, until well risen and golden brown. Remove from the oven and leave to cool.

To finish, cut the scones horizontally in half, or simply pull them apart. Spread some jam over each half, then top with a small dollop of clotted cream. Hull the strawberries and cut them into quarters. With their tips pointing outwards place strawberry quarters, skin-side up, on the cream on the base of each scone, then cover with the scone top. Cut out the template of a cross, using a piece of card or the lid of a plastic container. Centre it on top of each scone and, using a small sieve or sugar shaker, dust lightly with the icing sugar. Carefully lift off the template.

Fun and
Festivities

Baby Shower Magic Cakes

Once you have mastered the Lemon Daisy Cakes on page 86, it's only one small step to tackling Konditor & Cook's signature Magic Cakes. A blank canvas for your creativity, they can be customised in every which way. A couple of tips: it is better to limit the colours – three or four different ones, or a suite of colour, always look very striking; and when making large arrangements, repeat some of the designs – not only is it easier, but also it has more impact. These baby shower magic cakes make a great gift, or could be used for a christening or first birthday cake.

At Konditor & Cook the cakes are dipped in baker's fondant – not to be confused with roll-out fondant or sugarpaste. Baker's fondant is a sugar coating that is solid in its cold state but becomes liquid when heated and diluted with water, lemon juice or alcohol. It is what bakers use to glaze Danish pastries. If you have a local baker, it's worth asking if they will sell you some, as I have never seen it in a shop. It is available online from Almond Art (www.almondart.com). If you can't get hold of baker's fondant, you could make a simpler but no less delicious version of these cakes by following the Lemon Daisy Cakes recipe on page 86, using pink colouring to dye the icing and applying the decorations as described here.

Makes 16–25

1 quantity of Lemon Sponge mixture (see page 86)

juice of 2 lemons

60g apricot glaze (or apricot jam, heated and strained through a sieve)

150g white marzipan

600g baker's fondant

pink and brown food colourings

1 quantity of Royal Icing (see page 211)

Bake the lemon sponge as described on page 86, then remove from the oven and leave to cool. Turn the sponge upside down and peel off the baking paper, then brush the juice of 1 lemon over the surface.

Warm the apricot glaze and brush half of it over the surface of the cake. Roll out the marzipan between 2 sheets of plastic (such as document wallets) into a square the same size as the cake. Carefully place the marzipan on the sponge and flatten it gently with the palm of your hand. Chill for 1 hour.

Remove the cake from the fridge, trim off the edges so you are left with a 20cm square, then cut it into 25 small (4cm x 4cm) or 16 slightly larger (5cm x 5cm) squares. Use a long serrated knife for this, making sure you wipe the blade clean between each cut to prevent the marzipan sticking. Reheat the remaining glaze and, with a plastic scraper or a palette knife, spread it in a thin layer over the marzipan. This will help the fondant maintain its glossy sheen. Refrigerate until ready to dip.

Continued...

Put the fondant in a small saucepan, add the remaining lemon juice and heat to 55°C, stirring constantly. Once it has reached the right temperature, add a little water to give a consistency like double cream. If you overheat the fondant, it will be very runny and lose its sheen on setting.

Now dip the cakes in varying shades of pink. Add a tiny amount of pink colouring to the fondant to give the palest shade, dip 4 or 5 cakes, then add a bit more pink colouring and dip another 4–5 cakes. Repeat until all are used up, setting the cakes down on a wire rack to dry as you do them. Be sure to dip the cakes marzipan-side down into the fondant. Only dip about a third of the way down the sides of each cake, as the fondant will run off and cover it further. Once the cakes are touch-dry, cut them loose from the wire rack and set them down in round paper or foil cake cases, gently pressing the case on to the sides of each cake so it sticks to it and takes on its shape.

Put a quarter of the royal icing in a small bowl and colour it brown. Put another quarter in a second bowl and leave it white. Cover with a lid or a damp cloth to prevent a skin forming. Turn the remainder into 'run-out' icing – icing with a runnier consistency – by stirring in a little water a few drops at a time until it has the consistency of custard.

Using small parchment piping bags (see page 216), pipe the outlines of toys, baby bottles or any letters in brown. Use the white to ice teddy bears, storks and details of toys. Once the outlines are dry, fill a small parchment piping bag with the run-out icing and fill the shapes in with it as if you were having fun with a colouring-in book. Leave to dry, then add further details, such as numbers or letters on the toys or a scale on the milk bottle.

'Spiders from Mars' Cupcakes

Will these creepy-crawly-topped cupcakes make you an arachnophobe or an arachnophile – trick or treat? Dark gingerbread sponge topped with a Halloween orange frosting is to die for! We call them Spiders from Mars because they are sitting on a 'red' planet of orange frosting.

The cupcakes and topping are dead easy to make. You can buy chocolate truffles or other round or oval chocolate shapes to make the spider's bodies, and use thin strands of liquorice for their legs (for me, definitely a 'trick' taste). Or go for the 'treat' version – shaping the bodies out of home-made truffles as described below.

Makes 12

1 quantity of Black Gingerbread (the sponge element only from the Sunken Pear and Black Gingerbread Cake on page 31)

1 quantity of Cream Cheese Frosting (see page 211), flavoured with the grated zest of 1 unwaxed orange

a little orange food colouring

For the chocolate spiders:

60ml single cream

200g dark chocolate (60 per cent cocoa solids), chopped

2 tbsp cocoa powder

Heat the oven to 165°C/Gas Mark 3. Line a muffin tray with 12 paper cupcake cases.

Divide the sponge mixture between the cupcake cases and bake for 25 minutes, or until a skewer inserted in the centre comes out clean. Remove from the oven and leave to cool completely.

Colour the frosting with a little orange food colouring. Transfer it to a piping bag fitted with a medium-sized star nozzle and cover the surface of each cupcake with a swirl of frosting, leaving a small border all round so that the sponge is still visible.

Drag a toothpick or skewer from the centre to the edge of the frosting (like a five-pointed starfish) to create a spider's nest look. Set the cupcakes aside.

For the spiders' bodies, you will need to make some cocoa-dusted truffles. Put the cream in a small saucepan and start to heat gently. Add 120g of the chocolate and heat, stirring occasionally, until the chocolate has melted and formed a smooth ganache. Remove from the heat, pour into a small, flat dish and leave to cool. Transfer to the fridge and leave for about 2 hours, until set.

Continued...

Dust a piece of baking parchment with half the cocoa powder. Use a teaspoon to divide the ganache into at least 12 truffle-sized portions. Roll them between your hands into rounds or ovals, or any spider body shape you fancy – if you don't like the chocolate melting on your hands you can wear latex gloves while doing this. Set the bodies on the cocoa-dusted paper, dust with the remaining cocoa powder and roll them around to give a 'hairy', velvety appearance. Set aside in the fridge.

To make the legs, gently melt the rest of the chocolate in a small Bowl set over a pan of hot water or in the microwave.

Line a baking tray with baking parchment. Make a few small piping bags out of baking parchment (see page 216). Fill one with a little melted chocolate (it will set quickly, so it's easiest to work with a little at a time; just move on to a new piping bag when necessary). Pipe 3mm-thick and 2cm-high V-hook shapes on to the parchment-lined tray. The bottom of the V-hook turned by 180 degrees will form the 'knee' of the spider's leg. You can influence the look by giving the sets of legs different angles. A wide-angled knee will make the spider straddle the cupcake like a daddy-long-legs. Remember that spiders have 8 legs, so you will need 96 for 12 cupcakes! Pipe plenty of spares, as they are fragile. Place the tray in the fridge to set the chocolate fully.

To assemble the spiders, place a spider's body in the centre of each cupcake. Using a knife, release the legs from the parchment, then carefully pick them up with your fingers and stick them into the frosting, 4 on each side of the spider's body, slightly tucking them under and fanning them out as spiders' legs do. At your first attempt, this may take some time. If the chocolate legs start to go soft, put them back in the fridge and continue once they have hardened.

Now that the bodies and legs are in place, give the spiders a little more character by making eyes. Use the blunt end of a skewer or similar instrument to make 2 small indents in each spider. They look cuter if they are quite close together and if you make them look in different directions.

Trick or treat? You will either be in love with spiders or hate them forever after completing these cupcakes! Ha ha ha...

Spaghetti Bolognese Cupcakes

Most kids love spaghetti Bolognese. It's a great-tasting dish and so wonderfully messy too. This is the sweet answer to the classic favourite. Ever so slightly surreal, these cupcakes could have been dreamed up by Dalí or Magritte, but in fact are the fruits of a little childlike imagination (always helpful when it comes to cakes).

Not at all savoury, they are made from Victoria sponge, mascarpone frosting, strawberry jam, plus some ground almonds standing in for Parmesan cheese.

Makes 12

1 quantity of Victoria
    Sponge Cake mixture
    (see page 17)

a little egg-yellow
    food colouring

1 quantity of Mascarpone
    Frosting, flavoured with
    vanilla (see page 213)

200g strawberry jam (or
    any red jam)

4 tbsp ground almonds

Heat the oven to 165°C/Gas Mark 3. Put 12 paper cupcake cases in a muffin tray.

Divide the sponge mixture between the cupcake cases, filling them three-quarters full. Bake for 25 minutes, until well risen and golden brown. Remove from the oven and leave to cool.

Add a little yellow colouring to the frosting to dye it a spaghetti-yellow shade. Since this is a bit of fun, I think it looks better with a hyper-realistic degree of colour rather than the cooked colour of real spaghetti. Make a parchment piping bag (see page 216) and cut a small hole in the end, or fit a plastic piping bag with a 2mm nozzle. Put a little of the frosting in the bag. It is hard to pipe very thin strands with a full piping bag, so opt for several refills – or use several small piping bags each filled with enough frosting for 2 or 3 cakes.

Pipe the frosting on each cupcake, working from the edge inwards, going round several times to build it up, then increasing the height to make it look as if the strands are twisting round a fork.

Pass the jam through a sieve to remove any obvious fruit pieces. Then pipe or place approximately a teaspoon of the jam on top of each mound of 'spaghetti'. Garnish with a sprinkling of ground almonds and serve with a cake fork – or disposable fork, if you have any – stuck in the top.

'Curly' the Woolly Sheep Cupcakes

Konditor & Cook's favourite recipe, the Curly Whirly Cake (see page 14), lends itself to making delicious cupcakes. The recipe really delivers on taste.

For a simple finish, sprinkle with chocolate shavings or piped chocolate swirls or, for a quick decorative solution, rely on bought cake sprinkles or edible glitter. If you want to go the extra mile, however, try these woolly sheep. It's simply a case of piping the frosting on in a curly, 'woolly' fashion, then hand crafting the marzipan heads with the aid of some implements you should be able to find in your kitchen. A little wonkiness adds charm and character. Give it a go!

Makes 12

1 quantity of Curly
Whirly Cake mixture
(see page 14)

1 quantity of Cream Cheese
Frosting, flavoured with
vanilla (see page 211)

For the sheep heads:

3 tbsp cocoa powder

200g white marzipan

3 tbsp cocoa powder

a little pink food colouring

Heat the oven to 180°C/Gas Mark 4. Put 12 paper cupcake cases in a muffin tray.

Divide the sponge mixture between the cupcake cases and bake for 20 minutes, until the sponge bounces back when pressed gently. Remove from the oven and leave to cool completely.

Put the frosting in a piping bag fitted with a 4mm plain nozzle. Pipe curly-whirly loops starting on the outside of each cupcake and overlapping the rounds as you go along. Hold back a small cupful of the frosting to make some curls on the sheep's forehead and to add the eyes and pink nose details.

Knead the cocoa powder into the marzipan until you have an evenly coloured paste. Divide it into 12 pieces roughly the size of quail's eggs for the sheep's heads and 24 smaller, coffee-bean-sized pieces for the ears, as well as some tiny 2mm balls for the eyes.

Model each larger piece into a head by rolling it into a ball using the flat of your hands, then into a pear shape between the sides of your hands. Place on a tray lined with baking parchment and flatten slightly. The narrower end will be the nose part. Using a skewer or the round end of a chopstick, make 2 indentations for the eye sockets.

Mould each coffee-bean-sized piece of marzipan into an almond shape, then indent the centre using the side of a skewer. Assemble the sheep on top of the cupcakes by putting a head in the centre of each cake and tucking the ears slightly underneath at the sides.

Add some piped details. Make a small parchment piping bag (see page 216), fill it with some of the reserved vanilla frosting and pipe some curls on the sheep's foreheads and a small round dot in each eye socket. Add one of the little balls of coloured marzipan to each eye to form the iris. Dye a little frosting pink, put it in another piping bag and pipe it on for the noses.

Velvet Bunny Cake

This cute little bunny will delight children, and not just at Easter time. Shaping the body is easy cake sculpting and needs more courage than technique. Things get a little messy when it comes to rolling, shaping and particularly dusting the velvety-looking fur made from chocolate marzipan and cocoa – all part of the fun, of course.

The bunny's head can be baked from gingerbread or some leftover sweet pastry. It looks best, though, in chocolate sablé pastry. If you had to bake a series of these cakes, a bunny-head-shaped cookie cutter would be handy but for a one-off you can easily improvise. Cut a template from paper or thick card first and trace round it with the tip of a knife. Or boldly cut the bunny out freestyle with a sharp, pointed knife. Use the long ears to give the bunny head some characteristic definition. A few hand-moulded pieces of marzipan as paws and tail add the finishing touches to the cake.

You will need to have all the individual components prepared before you start assembling the cake. This includes the sponge, ganache filling, chocolate marzipan, white marzipan tail, the biscuit head, and royal icing for the piped details.

½ quantity of Victoria
  Sponge Cake mixture
  (see page 17)

1 quantity of Chocolate
  Sablé Pastry
  (see page 206)

350g white marzipan

a little white food
  colouring (optional)

4 tbsp cocoa powder, sifted

a little Royal Icing
  (see page 211)

1 quantity of Truffle
  Ganache (see page 212)

a little icing sugar,
  for dusting

Bake the sponge cake in a 20cm sandwich tin following the instructions on page 17. Remove from the oven and leave to cool.

For the biscuit head, about a third of the sablé pastry will probably suffice. However, it is safer to bake a couple extra, just in case of breakages. Roll out the pastry on a lightly floured surface to 4mm thick and, using a template or a small paring knife, cut out the head. The face should be a slightly oval shape about 9cm in diameter. The ears should be about 10cm long and 3–4 cm at their widest part. It's better to cut the head and ears from one piece of pastry, as if you join them together it is likely to break. Place on a parchment-lined baking tray and bake at 190°C/Gas Mark 5 for 9–10 minutes, until just firm to the touch. Remove from the oven and leave to cool.

Cut off a matchbox-sized piece of marzipan for the tail and leave it natural or dye it white by kneading a little white colouring into it. Mould it into a short carrot shape, pointy at one end and round at the other, and set aside.

Make the rest of the marzipan into chocolate marzipan by kneading 2 teaspoons of water into it followed by 3 tablespoons of the sifted cocoa powder. Wrap in cling film and set aside.

You will need only a small parchment piping bag (see page 216) of royal icing.

Continued...

You can follow the recipe on page 211 and keep the rest of the icing in the fridge, or you could improvise by sifting a cupful of icing sugar into a bowl and adding enough egg white (about 1 teaspoon) to mix it into a thick paste. Ice the facial details on the biscuit and leave to dry. Give the bunny some dark pupils by rolling 2 tiny balls of chocolate marzipan into coffee-bean-shaped ovals and attaching them.

To assemble the cake, slice the sponge horizontally in half, cut out a 13cm-diameter disc (use a saucer as a template) from each layer and sandwich them together with some of the ganache. Cover the top with ganache, then, using a small blob of ganache, fix the discs on to a cake board or flat plate – this is to prevent the sponge moving when you dust off the cocoa powder later.

Roughly break up the rest of the sponge, put it in a small bowl and mix it with 4 heaped tablespoons of ganache. Pile on top of the sponge base and shape into a dome. Add a little more ganache and smooth the sides. Cover with cling film and squeeze the cake into more of an oval shape with your hands. Place in the fridge and leave to set for 1 hour. Remove from the fridge and cover with a final thick layer of soft ganache.

To make the velvet fur, roll the chocolate marzipan out between 2 sheets of plastic (such as document wallets) into a circle 2mm thick and 30–35cm in diameter. Dust a metal disc or upturned baking tray with a little icing sugar and place the marzipan sheet, with the plastic removed, on top. Mould it into waves, then slide it over the domed cake, tucking it in around the sides. Trim off the excess and set aside for the paws; you will need 2 roughly walnut-sized pieces.

Evenly dust the top of the cake with the remaining cocoa powder, then shake off the excess by holding the cake slightly sideways and tapping it from underneath. Now transfer it to another cake board or serving dish to finish.

Mould the bunny's paws by shaping the reserved marzipan into 2 long lozenges. Use a skewer to mark the claws. Place the paws at the front of the cake, where the head will go. Using your finger or the end of a knife, make a hole at the bunny's back and then insert the tail.

Finally, place the bunny's head on top of the paws, leaning it against the body. To make it more secure, mark a small groove in the top of the paws so it can't slide off.

Chocolate Cabbage

I'm hoping you will have baked your way through the book before you land on this page. At this point you definitely deserve to attempt this chocolate extravaganza. The idea came from a challenge set a few years ago by Priscilla Carluccio, sister of Sir Terence Conran. She has often provided us with great cake challenges, including themed cakes for family birthday celebrations – sculpted, tiered, layered, cakes in all shapes and sizes. One year a cabbage cake was requested and, rather than icing a picture of a cabbage on a cake, we decided to make one in chocolate.

I'm very grateful to Priscilla for giving me the opportunity to create some truly wonderful one-off work, including her brother's eightieth birthday cake, which was so tall it deserves a book of instructions all of its own (see page 6).

The most difficult aspect of this chocolate cabbage is tempering the chocolate. The rest just needs nerves and a kitchen capable of handling an unusually large amount of chocolate. Rather than making the whole cabbage, you could experiment with a few single leaves first. They make very beautiful edible serving dishes for chocolate truffles or individual desserts.

Cleaning up a chocolate-covered kitchen might seem like hard work, but you will be rewarded with the biggest cheers ever upon presenting this cake to an audience. Have a go – it's worth it.

½ quantity of Dark Chocolate Sponge mixture (see page 14)

1 quantity of Truffle Ganache (see page 212)

1 medium-sized Savoy cabbage

3 tbsp vegetable oil or sunflower oil

1.2kg dark chocolate (70 per cent cocoa solids) – allow 120–150g chocolate per leaf

Inside the chocolate cabbage is a small, ball-shaped cake on to which the leaves are stuck. Bake the sponge mixture in a 17cm sandwich tin according to the instructions on page 14 and leave to cool (or you could bake the full quantity of the mixture and serve the second layer as a small cake on the side).

Cut the sponge into 3cm cubes and place in a mixing bowl. Add half the ganache and mix with a spatula until the cake is evenly coated; you should still be able to see chunks of cake rather than mixing it to a pulp. Line a cereal bowl or similar half-sphere bowl with cling film and fill with the cake mix, building it up into a sphere. Cover the dome with more cling film and smooth the sides. Chill for at least 2 hours, until set.

Prepare the cabbage leaves next. You will need about 8, plus a few extra in case there are any breakages. Discard the very outer leaves of the cabbage, as they may be contaminated with soil. Inspect the others thoroughly and give them a quick wipe with kitchen paper on the side you take the imprint from. On a cabbage you actually see the underside of each leaf, therefore you have to make the imprint from the other side.

Continued...

Let's say you were practising or wanted to make a single leaf dish on which to serve some truffles (as you do), then you would want to see the top of the leaf and make the imprint from the underside. Brush the top of the leaves thinly and evenly with the oil, making sure you get it into all the nooks and crannies.

It is really important that the chocolate you use for coating the leaves is tempered, otherwise it will not separate from the cabbage leaves. Temper it following the instructions on page 217.

When the chocolate is correctly tempered, remove the cake ball from the fridge and take off the cling film. Place the cake on a cake board or a dish you can work on. The cabbage will look better if you can't see the cake, so the first 2 leaves should be used to cover the ball and be set directly on the cabbage, thus hugging the shape. They should overlap slightly at the top. Therefore set one leaf first before adding the second.

Begin by brushing chocolate on to one of the inner leaves, using a pastry brush. Make sure you get the chocolate into all the cavities. Now mould the chocolate-covered leaf on to the cake ball. Since the ball is cold from the fridge, the chocolate should set quite quickly. Once it is hard, carefully peel off the actual cabbage leaf from the top down. Now brush a second leaf with chocolate and place it, slightly overlapping at the top, opposite the first one. If parts of the leaves break off, stick the pieces together with ganache.

The outer leaves need to be finished individually and stuck on afterwards. To give them strength and stability, they are coated in 2 layers of chocolate. Brush with one layer first and place in the fridge to set, then add a second layer. It is easier to peel the green cabbage leaves off if the chocolate leaves are set really hard. Once all the leaves are set, carefully remove the real cabbage leaves by peeling them away from the thin parts towards the centre, which should be thicker. This minimises the risk of their breaking. Soften the remainder of the ganache or use leftover melted chocolate to stick the leaves on to the central core. Start with the smaller leaves and work your way outwards with the larger leaves.

Store the chocolate cabbage at room temperature. It does not need refrigerating and will keep for up to 10 days in cool, dry conditions. To serve, simply break off the leaves, then cut the central cake.

Gingerbread Grannies

This gingerbread dough is a fantastic recipe that can be used to make a wide range of decorative cookies and characters – Christmas tree hangings, gingerbread houses, edible gift tags, or just a large batch of gingerbread people so you can have some decorating fun with the kids. Throughout the year we celebrate different events at Konditor & Cook and these gingerbread grannies, seemingly taking off on a trip around the world, are an example of how you can customise a regular gingerbread shape by adding a little extra dough to create an extension for their hair or cut-out bags and suitcases.

This recipe is very reliable and makes quite a malleable dough, easy for children to use too. You can freeze it if you don't use it all. In fact it's quite good to have some in your freezer portioned up into smaller batches so you only have to defrost a little if it's just a single biscuit you are after – such as the wood saw for the Black Forest Yule Log on page 194. Have fun!

Makes 12–16 biscuits

For the gingerbread dough:

150g light soft brown sugar

4 tbsp golden syrup

2 tbsp black treacle

1 tbsp ground cinnamon

1 tbsp ground ginger

a pinch of ground cloves

**grated zest of
1 unwaxed orange**

**175g salted butter,
cut into cubes**

1 tsp bicarbonate of soda

400g plain flour, sifted

To decorate:

**1 quantity of Royal Icing
(see page 211)**

Put the sugar, syrup, treacle, spices and orange zest in a pan, add 2 tablespoons of water and bring to the boil, stirring to dissolve the sugar. Remove from the heat and stir in the butter until melted. Mix in the bicarbonate of soda and then add the flour while the mixture is still warm. Remove the dough from the pan, wrap it in cling film and chill for at least an hour. It will keep in the fridge for up to a week.

Heat the oven to 180°C/Gas Mark 4. Roll out the dough on a lightly floured surface to 4–5mm thick. Cut out the shapes with a gingerbread cutter, then add extra pieces to create the hair extensions. I usually look for suitable offcuts, or I use the gingerbread cutter to cut away some sections – large plain piping nozzles are good for round shapes. Attach them to the gingerbread grannies by slightly overlapping the pieces and gently pressing them down. Animate the figures by moving the arms up and down so that they look less like robots and more like fun-loving grannies. Cut out additional accessories – bags, suitcases – and attach these to the figures as well. If you feel very creative, cut out some pets too.

Continued...

CORRESPONDANCE
ADRESSE
Ce côté est exclusivement réservé à l'adresse
POSTKARTE
TARJETA POSTAL
CARTE POSTALE
CHEQUES POSTAUX
DEMANDEZ L'OUVERTURE
D'UN COMPTE COURANT
PARIS
SAINT-ROCH
CARTE POSTALE
Ce côté est exclusivement réservé à l'adre
Madame
STALE
CARTE POSTALE
Correspondance
CARTE POSTALE

Place on a baking tray lined with baking parchment and bake for about 15 minutes, until they are evenly dark brown and firm. Remove from the oven and leave to cool on the tray. If you want to make a very dry gingerbread – for example if you want to hang the grannies from your Christmas tree or if you are using this recipe to make other pendants or a gingerbread house – it is better to bake it twice: remove it from the oven, leave to cool for 15 minutes, then return to the oven for 5–10 minutes, depending on thickness.

To decorate the grannies, make a small parchment piping bag (see page 216) and fill with a walnut-sized portion of royal icing (keep any surplus icing in a sealed box in the fridge for up to 2 weeks, or freeze it). Using sharp scissors, cut a 2mm opening in the tip.

Pipe the eyes and mouth on the grannies first, followed by the outfits, hair and other details. Pay particular attention to the mouth and eyes. Simple dots for eyes are fine as long as they wear spectacles, otherwise make the eyes oval shaped and pipe them quite close together. Take your cue from Mickey Mouse. Give them a big smile for extra character! These sassy grannies will hopefully be the start of lots of gingerbread decorating fun.

Rainbow Dots
Lemon Chiffon Cake

After the Curly Whirly Cake (see page 14), the Lemon Chiffon is Konditor & Cook's most popular celebration cake. Lemon pleases those who like their cakes less sweet and rich. It's a favourite with adults as well as children, and it can be washed down equally well with tea, coffee or champagne.

The decorations on this cake are inspired by a universally liked symbol – the rainbow. You can't go wrong choosing this design for a celebration cake, be it a birthday or some other happy occasion. Piping a series of dots is a great way to create an impact on a cake. And you can do it without needing to acquire a lot of decorating skills. All you need is some royal icing, piping bags, food colouring and edible glitter.

The marzipan dots around the base of the cake are an optional extra. The choice of cake stand or additional decoration is an important element that contributes to the overall presentation of a cake. To give this one the wow factor, we continued the dotty theme by placing irregular-sized marzipan dots around the perimeter of the cake stand.

Makes a 17cm cake

1 quantity of Lemon
   Sponge mixture
   (see page 86)

50g caster sugar

juice of 2 lemons

1 quantity of Cream
   Cheese Frosting,
   flavoured with lemon
   (see page 211)

1 quantity of Royal Icing
   (see page 211)

food colourings of
   your choice

a little edible glitter

100–150g white marzipan
   (or sugarpaste) (optional)

a little pearl lustre dust
   (optional)

Heat the oven to 165°C/Gas Mark 3. Divide the lemon sponge mixture between 2 buttered and flour-dusted 17cm sandwich tins and bake for about 25 minutes, until a skewer inserted in the centre comes out clean. Leave to cool in the tins for 10 minutes, then turn out on to a wire rack to cool completely.

To make a lemon syrup, put the caster sugar in a small saucepan with 50ml water and bring to the boil, stirring to dissolve the sugar. Remove from the heat, leave to cool for a few minutes, then add the lemon juice.

With a serrated cake knife, cut each cake in half horizontally. The trick is not simply to cut from one side to the other, as this can result in uneven layers, but to put one hand flat on top of the sponge while you cut. Using a sawing motion, just move the knife back and forth, slowly spinning the sponge with the other hand. In this way you will gradually cut to the centre of the sponge. Place the cake layers cut-side up on a baking tray or a board and evenly apply the lemon syrup with a pastry brush.

Continued...

There are 2 options for layering the cake, one rustic, the other more refined. For a simple version, leave the sides exposed and just layer the sponges with the frosting. In this case, use a palette knife to spread a quarter of the lemon frosting on to each layer.

For a more elegant finish, you need to cover the sides of the cake with frosting too. Keep the filling layers quite thin, stack up the cakes and spread a first thin layer of frosting over the top and sides to bind the crumbs, using a palette knife. Chill the cake for 1 hour, then spread the rest of the frosting over the top and down the sides. If you use a cake turntable, give it a spin at the end with the tip of the palette knife pressed on to the top of the cake to create a spiral swirl. Place the cake in the fridge to set.

Divide the royal icing into 6 portions if using 6 separate food colourings. Alternatively, you can mix the colours of the rainbow from just 3 base colours, red, yellow and blue. Yellow combined with blue will make green, while red and blue become purple. When mixing colours, it is not simply a case of mixing equal parts; sometimes just a touch of blue will make a red go purple. Likewise a tiny touch of blue should turn yellow into green. Colourings vary in concentration, tone and consistency – it really is a case of awakening your inner Matisse.

Make 6 parchment piping bags (see page 216), snip a 3mm hole in the end of each one and fill with the coloured icings. Start by piping a string of about 12 dots in a single colour around the centre of the cake. Then pipe another colour next, placing each dot in a gap of the previous circle. Repeat this with the remaining colours. This way you will pipe the same amount of dots for each colour and the cake becomes lighter towards the edge, adding a certain dynamic. If you pipe strings of dots in circles you will need more icing for the longer outer rings than for the inner rings.

For a bit of sparkle, apply a little edible glitter to each dot. Depending on the make, some glitters stick to the skin and can be dabbed on using your index finger. Others are better applied using a small brush.

To incorporate the cake board or plate into the design, repeat the dot idea using marzipan. Divide the marzipan into 6 and knead a small amount of the food colourings used for the icing into each one. Roll out the pieces to 2–3mm thick between 2 sheets of plastic (such as document wallets). Using small, round pastry cutters or large piping nozzles, cut out circles varying in size from 1cm to 3cm. Brush each with a little glitter or some pearl lustre dust and arrange in a random pattern around the cake.

Mulled Wine Cupcakes

Once upon a time there were just fairy cakes and butterfly cakes. Then along came *Sex and the City*, featuring New York's Magnolia Bakery. Since then cupcakes have taken the world by storm and helped to make baking sexy in the process. Imagine the famous Christmas tree at the Rockefeller Center and Carrie and Co luxuriating with these mulled wine cups while taking a well-deserved break from their Christmas shopping extravaganza.

To rewind TV history, you will need…

Makes 12

1 quantity of Henrietta's Tipsy Cake mixture (see page 27), with the following items added:

grated zest of 1 unwaxed orange

¼ tsp ground nutmeg

a pinch of ground cloves

For the marzipan glitter star decorations:

50g white marzipan

a little food colouring – traditional Christmas red or a funky pink or purple

edible glitter to match the colour

For the spiced mascarpone frosting:

1 quantity of Mascarpone Frosting (see page 213), flavoured with ½ tsp ground mixed spice and ½ tsp ground cinnamon

Alternative decoration:

candied orange zest, made following the method in Carrot and Walnut Cupcakes (see page 161)

It's best to make the decorations a day in advance. This will give them a chance to dry out and help them to stand up on the cakes. Dye the marzipan by adding a little food colouring to it and kneading it in until evenly distributed. Roll the marzipan out between 2 sheets of plastic (such as document wallets) until it is 2mm thick. Cut out the stars with a small cookie star cutter, then dip one side of each star in the edible glitter. Place on a tray lined with baking parchment and leave to dry.

Heat the oven to 165°C/Gas Mark 3. Line a muffin tin with 12 paper cupcake cases.

Divide the sponge mixture between the cupcake cases and bake for 25 minutes, until they are well risen and a skewer inserted in the centre comes out clean. Remove from the oven and leave to cool completely.

Make a parchment piping bag (see page 216) and cut a hole in the end, or fit a plastic piping bag with a 1cm nozzle. Pipe the frosting over the cupcakes, leaving a small gap around the edge so that the sponge is visible. To pipe a Christmas tree, cut a 3mm hole in the parchment piping bag, or fit a plastic piping bag with a 3mm plain nozzle. Build up the tree by piping short 'branches' on top of one another – rather like stacking a series of starfish. Start the piping in the centre, then, as you pipe outwards, reduce the pressure and drag the piping bag away to give each branch a tapered look. Reduce the length towards the top.

Put the cupcakes in the fridge to set the frosting, then add the star decorations to the top. If using candied orange zest to decorate, pipe swirls of frosting on each cake and loosely drape a few strands of zest over the top.

Dodgy Jammers

At Konditor & Cook, playfulness and humour play a big part, and here it's a play on words. These are not the classic, mass-produced British biscuits with a hole in the middle. These contain cheeky baked messages that will make them the talk of your tea party. They are perfect for your first steps in baking. And, combined with your own wit, they can make a cheeky gift too.

Our inspiration came from the Valentine's theme, 'Love is a four-letter word'. We had made heart-shaped jammy dodgers in the past but this time we thought we'd revert to a round biscuit and use an alphabet cutter set to make our four-letter words. I never knew there were so many words in the English language that could be accommodated on a biscuit: LOVE, TART, SEXY, KISS, FART were some of the more printable words our cake decorators and bakers associated with Valentine's Day (and our customers requested). Some were well dodgy, and that's what gave the humble jammy dodger a new name – Dodgy Jammer.

Makes 4 large jammers

1 quantity of Sweet Pastry (see page 206)

120g raspberry jam

Heat the oven to 180°C/Gas Mark 4. Line a baking sheet with baking parchment.

Remove the pastry from the fridge, knead it briefly by hand, then roll out on a lightly floured work surface to about 3mm thick.

Cut out 8 discs using a 13cm crinkled cutter – or a plain saucer if you don't have a cutter. Re-roll the trimmings, if necessary, in order to cut out more discs.

With small alphabet cutters, cut out letters/words of your choosing in half the discs. Be careful not to leave too small a space between each letter, as thin bits of pastry will burn before the thicker parts are cooked.

Place the discs on the lined baking tray, spacing them 1cm apart. Bake for about 15 minutes, until they are a yellow-gold colour. Remove from the oven and leave to cool.

To finish, heat the raspberry jam (be careful, as it can get very hot). Turn each solid biscuit upside down, as the base is usually the flatter surface and this stops the biscuits breaking when sandwiched together. Spread with about 2 tablespoons of the hot jam. Place a lettered biscuit on top and gently press into place. There should be enough jam on the base to fill in the letters slightly when you do this. The biscuits will stay crisp for a few days if kept in an airtight tin. They will become a little softer as time goes on, but should keep for up to a month.

White Chocolate Coconut Macaroons

In Germany this kind of macaroon would be baked around Christmas time. I think they taste just as good all year round and make a great addition to a teatime selection.

Sandwiched with a fine piping of clotted cream and filled with raspberry jam, they make a jewel-like sweet canapé. With a few currants and flaked almonds, they can be transformed into creatures that will thrill children at a birthday party.

Makes about 60 singles
or 30 sandwiches

150g white chocolate

200g desiccated coconut

4 medium egg whites

a pinch of salt

150g caster sugar

For sandwiching:

100g raspberry jam

100g clotted cream (or a
little Mascarpone
Frosting, see page 213)

To make chipmunks
or mice:

50g flaked almonds

50g currants

25g dark chocolate

Heat the oven to 180°C/Gas Mark 4. Chop the white chocolate into very small pieces (about 2–3mm), then mix with the desiccated coconut.

Put the egg whites in a large bowl with the salt, and whisk with an electric mixer until bubbles form. Gradually, spoon by spoon, whisk in the caster sugar until you have a soft-peaked meringue. Using a spatula, gently fold in the chocolate coconut mix.

Pipe or spoon heaps of the mixture, roughly 2cm in diameter, on to a baking sheet lined with baking parchment. Bake for 10–12 minutes, until they just turn slightly golden. They brown very quickly, usually on the base first, so keep an eye on them.

Remove from the oven and leave to cool, then carefully lift them off the baking parchment. They are very moreish served plain, but make an afternoon-tea treat sandwiched together with clotted cream and raspberry jam – simply spread the base of one macaroon with jam, another with clotted cream, and press them together. Or, if you wish to add a little more detail, pipe the cream around the perimeter rather than spreading it.

You could also style the macaroons like animals for a children's party. To make chipmunks, keep the macaroons round; to make mice, pipe them in a teardrop shape. Insert the pointy end of 2 flaked almonds as ears and add 2 currants as eyes, then bake as above. Melt the chocolate, put it into a small parchment piping bag (see page 216), then pipe the nose detail on to their faces.

Black Forest Yule Log

We took our inspiration for this from the lovely light bark of silver birch trees, combined with the flavours found in a Black Forest gâteau. Coming from Freiburg, I was practically born with a spoonful of Black Forest gâteau in my mouth. The gâteau is traditionally filled with whipped cream, and you could easily use this to replace the buttercream here. However, if you are making this cake to be a Christmas table centrepiece, buttercream has the advantage of staying fresh longer.

The chocolate sponge is a flour-free recipe suitable for those on a wheat- or gluten-free diet. Making the marzipan decorations is quite simple, even if you have never attempted them before. You don't need any specialist equipment – a holly leaf cutter helps, but even without that you can simply cut the leaves out freestyle. The wood saw is an optional extra, baked from some leftover gingerbread dough (see page 182) and decorated with melted chocolate.

For the chocolate sponge:

100g dark chocolate
(70 per cent cocoa
solids), chopped

4 medium eggs, separated

a pinch of salt

120g caster sugar

icing sugar, for dusting

For the filling and finish:

2 tbsp kirsch

1 quantity of Quick
Buttercream, flavoured
with white chocolate
(see page 212)

200g sour cherries,
available in jars or frozen

For the decoration:

25g dark chocolate

75g white marzipan

green and red
food colourings

Heat the oven to 180°C/Gas Mark 4. Line a 30cm x 40cm baking tray with baking parchment.

Melt the chocolate in a bowl set over a pan of gently simmering water or in a microwave.

Put the egg whites in a large, very clean mixing bowl, add the salt and start whisking them slowly until they begin to go frothy. Now add a few tablespoons of the caster sugar and increase the speed of the beater. Gradually increase the amount of sugar you add and take the mixer up to maximum speed. The whites should be whipped to soft peaks, with a silky, white appearance.

Add the yolks to the meringue and briefly whisk them in. Now take a whiskful of the meringue and fold it into the melted chocolate (this is so both mixes have roughly the same consistency). Add the chocolate mix to the remaining meringue mixture and fold it in until it has a mousse-like appearance.

Pour the mixture into the lined baking tray and use a spatula or palette knife to coax it into the corners. Bake for 10–12 minutes; the sponge usually has a very thin, brittle crust but is soft and malleable when baked. Remove from the oven and leave to cool in the tray.

To remove the sponge from the tray, take a piece of baking parchment slightly longer than the baking tray and dust it with icing sugar.

Continued...

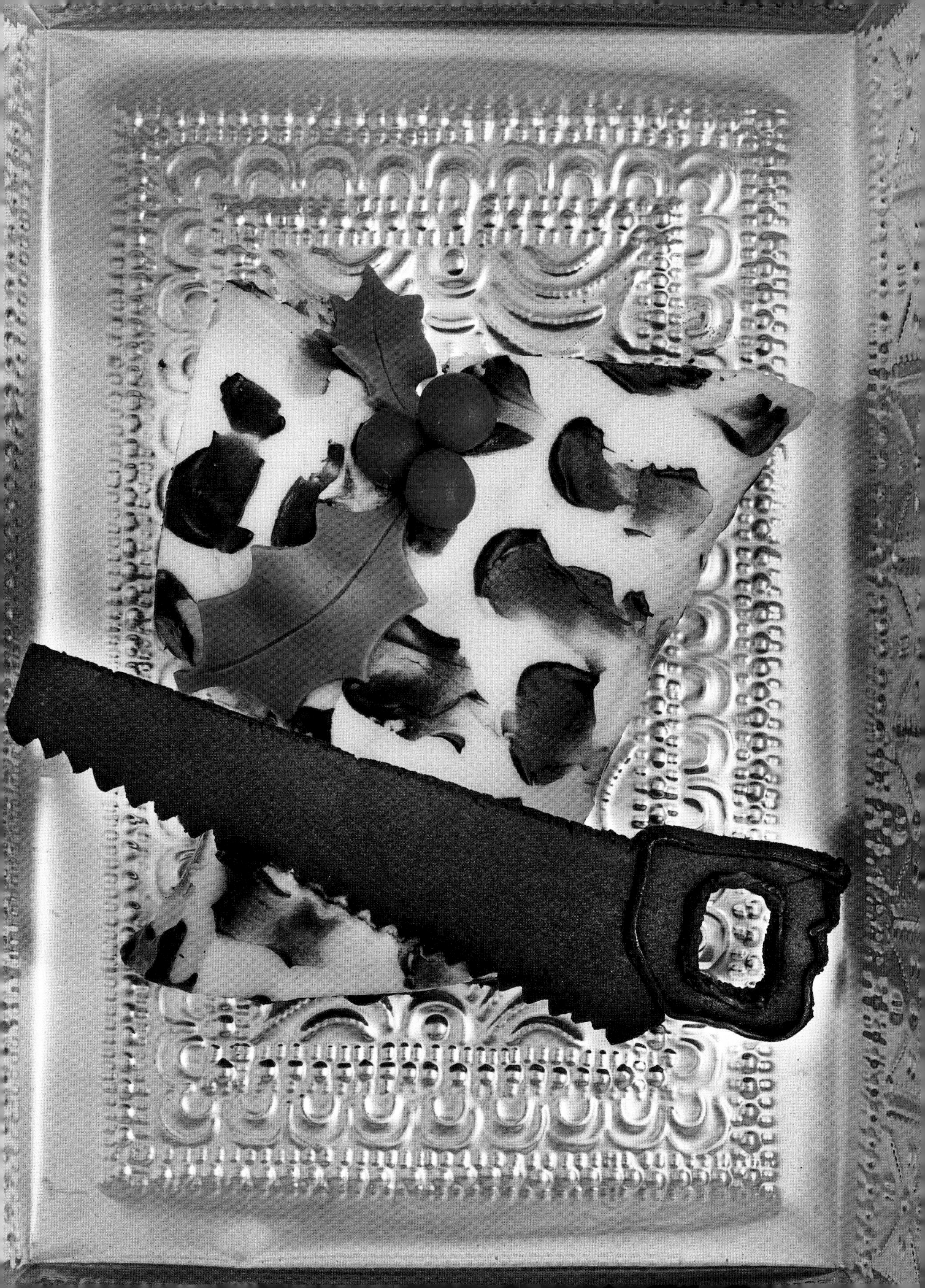

Using both hands, pick up 2 corners of the paper lining the tray and flip the sponge upside down on to the sugar-dusted parchment. Peel the backing paper off the sponge. It's best to work from inside to outside to stop the edges breaking. Cut a slit in the middle of the paper with a small knife, then slowly peel it off, moving towards the edges of the sponge.

To make the filling, mix a tablespoon of the kirsch into the buttercream to give it the Black Forest touch. Drain or defrost the cherries and briefly marinate them in the remaining tablespoon of kirsch.

Spread the sponge with two-thirds of the buttercream in an even layer. Orientate the sponge so that you are looking at it in portrait format. Place a row of cherries along the top end, to make sure every slice will include a bite of the cherry. Sprinkle the remainder of the cherries over the rest of the sponge.

To roll it up, pick up the 2 top corners of the paper and start 'pulling' them towards you, thus rolling up the sponge. Now don't panic if this doesn't work first time round. I once had the pleasure of demonstrating this method on *The Paul O'Grady Show* and then challenged actress Celia Imrie to copy it in 2 minutes. Let's just say it provided a great comic moment. The trick is to keep your hands low while pulling. The lower they are, the tighter the roll will be, and the higher they are the looser it will roll up. When you come to the end, let the roll tip over so that it rests on its seam. Remove any paper and transfer the roll to a chopping board or flat baking tray to make the finishing easier.

To make the decoration, melt the dark chocolate in a small bowl set over a pan of hot water or in the microwave. Using a small palette knife, cover the roll with the rest of the buttercream. Then make the side branch by cutting off a 4cm piece on the diagonal. Using a little buttercream, stick it on to the side of the log, then tidy up the join.

Give the log a bark-like texture by running the tip of your palette knife along the buttercream to make long grooves. Once you are happy with the design, dip the end of the palette knife into the melted dark chocolate and, with a forward movement, dab on chocolate highlights. A little streakiness will give it an authentic look. (If you plan to make the gingerbread saw, save a little chocolate for decorating it.)

Now make the marzipan decorations. Dye two-thirds of the marzipan a holly-green colour, adding a little green colouring to it and kneading it in until evenly distributed. Dye the rest of the marzipan red. Roll the green marzipan out between 2 sheets of plastic (such as document wallets) to 2–3mm thick and cut out 2 large holly leaves, either with a leaf cutter or freestyle. Using the back of a small knife, mark the midrib into the leaves to give them some texture. Roll the red marzipan into small balls to make holly berries.

Place the leaves on the log in a slightly bent fashion, using them to hide the connection with the branch. Add the holly berries for the finishing touch.

To make the wood saw, roll out 150g of the gingerbread dough (see page 182) and cut out a saw, roughly 15–20cm x 6–10cm – you can make a template out of paper first, if you like, and trace round it with a knife. Bake it following the instructions for Gingerbread Grannies on page 182. Pipe a few details on the handle with 25g melted dark chocolate.

Dark Chocolate Birthday Cake

Every now and then, a special birthday calls for a large celebration cake that will feed a greater number of guests. Cake portions can vary hugely, from 50g in a party scenario to around 100g for a dessert portion. At a party, a little can go a long way. This double-layered 22cm square cake could feed a greedy 20 or a more modest 40.

If you are giving a party for 40 guests, the cake should somehow keep up in proportion to the party. Rather than baking a cake of humungous size, it is sometimes better to stick to a smaller cake but surround it with a decorative frame on a larger cake board. This dark chocolate cake was placed on a 32cm board for the photo. The colourful fringe adds drama and makes it a cake fit for a special birthday moment. If you decide to make a shallower cake for half the number of people, use a single quantity of the sponge and ganache, but remember that the quantity of decoration needed will stay the same.

Many less experienced cake decorators find writing on a cake quite daunting. It requires a steady hand and an eye for balancing and spacing the writing. With these easy iced biscuits spelling out a name or message, you can make the decorations separately, discarding any that go wrong. Compose the design 'off cake' and, once you are happy, get ready to transfer them on to the cake.

2 quantities of Dark Chocolate Sponge mixture (see page 14)

1 quantity of Sweet Pastry (see page 206)

2 quantities of Truffle Ganache (see page 212)

360g white marzipan

pink, purple, orange and brown food colourings (or use colours of your choice)

1 quantity of Royal Icing (see page 211)

Divide the chocolate sponge mixture between two 22cm square cake tins, bake as described on page 14, then leave to cool.

Heat the oven to 190°C/Gas Mark 5. Roll out the sweet pastry on a lightly floured surface to 3mm thick and cut out biscuits. To write 'Happy Birthday', you will need 13 round biscuits made with a 3.5cm cutter. To cover the cake, you will need a further 10–12 shapes, such as flowers or hearts or even just round biscuits of varying sizes. Always bake a few spares in case the composition needs adjusting. Place the biscuits on a baking tray lined with baking parchment and bake for about 10 minutes, until golden brown. Remove from the oven and leave to cool.

To assemble the cake, trim the sides of the sponges to make them perfectly vertical. Spread the ganache over one of the cakes and sandwich them together. Coat the top and sides with a thin layer of ganache to bind any crumbs, then chill for 30 minutes. Remove from the fridge and coat with the remaining ganache, gently reheating the ganache first to soften it, if necessary. Save a little ganache for attaching the biscuits to the cake. Chill the cake for at least 30 minutes, until the ganache is set, then transfer to the centre of a 32cm square cake drum (a very sturdy cake board).

Continued...

Divide the marzipan into 3 blocks and dye them pink, purple and orange, kneading a little colouring into each one until evenly distributed.

You could use your own choice of colours instead, but bear in mind that it is better to limit the colours to a suite rather than mix too many different ones.

Roll out each piece of marzipan between 2 sheets of plastic (such as document wallets) and cut into bunting triangles – you will need about 15 in each colour. Their length is determined by the gap between the cake and the edge of board. Arrange them in a pattern around the base of the cake.

To finish the biscuits, divide the royal icing into 5 portions. Leave one white, then colour one brown and the others pink, orange and purple. Cover with a lid or a damp cloth to prevent a skin forming. Fill a small parchment piping bag (see page 216) with brown icing and outline the biscuits and any details. The outline will prevent the icing running over the edge of the biscuits. Leave to dry for 15 minutes. Stir a few drops of water into the remainder of each icing until it has a runny, custard-like consistency. Put a small amount of each icing in a parchment piping bag and fill in the shapes as if you were colouring in a picture. Leave for at least 30 minutes, until dry to the touch.

Outline the letters on the round biscuits and leave to dry for a further 30 minutes before filling them in with white. If you fill in the white too soon, there is the possibility that the colours will bleed into each other.

Arrange the biscuits off the cake first, then stick them on once you are happy with the layout. Using biscuits has the advantage that you can cantilever the decorations over the edge, making the cake look bigger and the design more relaxed and fun. Fill a piping bag with the remaining ganache and pipe 1cm-diameter blobs on to the cake on to which you can stick the biscuits. This elevates them, giving the cake height, and creates shadows that make it look more interesting.

Rocky Road Halloween Grave

Halloween, until recently celebrated more in America than anywhere else, is now being celebrated with great enthusiasm in other countries too. Themed parties are all the rage, so celebrate in style by adding some ghoulish food to your party, such as this spooky rocky road grave.

Rocky road is America's answer to chocolate biscuit cake. It only takes two changes to the basic recipe on page 42 to create this dish to end all diets. And all the decorations are made with marzipan, requiring no piping skills. Even the tombstone is engraved, as it should be (with the end of a skewer, no less), rather than inscribed. For the other decorations, you just need a couple of items that can be found in most kitchens, such as a garlic crusher and a sieve.

Make the tombstone a day in advance, as it will stand up better if it has had a chance to dry.

200g white marzipan

black, white and green food colourings

1 quantity of Chocolate Biscuit Cake mixture (see page 42), with the Brazil nuts replaced by 50g white mini marshmallows (or large marshmallows, cut into thirds)

1 tbsp cocoa powder

a little melted chocolate (to set the tombstone)

First colour the marzipan and make the decorations – it is better to shape the bones and tombstone well in advance and leave them to dry. Dye about 90g of the marzipan grey for the tombstone, using a little black colouring and kneading it into the marzipan until evenly distributed. Divide the remaining marzipan into 3 and dye one piece white, to shape into some loosely scattered bones, one piece light green and the final piece in a darker green.

Roll the grey marzipan out into a 1.5cm-thick rectangular block, giving it a slightly arched top. Use the blunt end of a skewer to engrave the letters. For the bones, roll the white marzipan into pieces 3–4 cm long with a thick epiphysis at either end, using the rounded side of a skewer to shape the thick ends. Make some smaller ones too, or try shaping a skeletal hand.

The grassy additions can be done in advance or made fresh. To shape the darker grass, take small lumps of dark green marzipan and press them through the mesh of a sieve. Use a small knife to cut off the 'turf' as it comes out on the other side. To shape the lighter, longer grass, press lumps of light green marzipan through a garlic crusher (a garlic crusher and a sieve are also good hair-making implements for some funky gingerbread people).

I use only about a third of the chocolate biscuit cake mixture to make the grave, but whatever you have left over can easily be set in a small dish lined with baking parchment. I'm sure it will not go to waste!

Continued...

To make the grave, line a small baking tray or rectangular dish with a sheet of baking parchment. Scoop the biscuit cake mixture on to the paper in a roughly 30cm x 15cm mounded shape. Where you want to set the tombstone, it helps to make an oblong hole and build up a bit of back support using some of the larger biscuit pieces in the mix. Overall there is no set rule to this: you can be as extravagant as you wish to be with your grave design! Once you are happy with the basic shape, place it in the fridge and leave for at least 3 hours or until set.

For the final assembly, remove the baking parchment from the base of the grave, and put it in its final resting place – an oblong dish, or a piece of slate perhaps. Dust lightly with the cocoa powder. Then set the tombstone in the cavity, using a little melted chocolate to stick it down, if necessary. Add the grass around the perimeter of the grave and the base of the tombstone, then scatter the bones over the top of the grave.

Basics, Tips and Techniques

Basics

Sweet Pastry

It's possible to cook savoury dishes without following a particular recipe. We all love chucking a few things in a pan and hoping we'll come out with something special at the other end. Baking, however, requires a degree of accuracy, otherwise it simply won't work. Not enough butter makes pastry tough, for example, while too much sugar will cause it to burn.

Some baking recipes are very easy to remember – a pound cake is simply equal weights of sugar, butter, eggs and flour. This pastry recipe is also quite easy, as it follows the ratio 1:2:3 – that's one part sugar to two parts butter and three parts flour, making six parts in total. From here on, you just need to work out how much pastry you need to line a pie tin or some tartlet cases to get you to the right quantity.

For a shorter texture, and to make the pastry easier to work with, I have included an egg yolk below. A tablespoon of milk would suffice if you don't have any eggs. Using salted butter gives the pastry more depth of flavour but if you have only unsalted butter available you can add a pinch of salt. Don't be tempted to substitute granulated sugar for caster, as the granulated sugar crystals are too large and will not give you evenly coloured pastry.

You can add flavourings to this pastry, if you like, such as a little lemon zest, vanilla or cinnamon.

50g caster sugar
1 medium egg yolk
100g salted butter, cut into cubes
150g plain flour

Put the sugar and egg yolk in a mixing bowl, combine briefly with a wooden spoon, then add the butter. Using the spoon or your fingers, blend them until they come together. You can also do this in a freestanding electric mixer. Sift in the flour and quickly work everything into a dough. Shape into a flat slab, wrap in cling film and chill for 1 hour before use. The pastry will keep in the fridge for 5 days and can also be frozen, well wrapped.

Sablé Pastry

(Vanilla and chocolate versions)
Sablé is the finest of all sweet pastries. It has the shortest texture and bakes evenly, making it particularly good for very fine tarts, dainty cookies or mini tartlets. Substitute caster sugar for icing sugar, if you wish, but not granulated.

Vanilla sablé:

100g unsalted butter, cut into cubes
1 medium egg yolk
50g icing sugar
¼ tsp vanilla extract
   or the seeds of ¼ vanilla pod
160g plain flour

Chocolate sablé:

100g unsalted butter, cut into cubes
1 medium egg yolk
50g icing sugar
140g plain flour
3 tbsp cocoa powder

Put the butter and egg yolk into a bowl and sift in the icing sugar – add the vanilla, too, if you are making vanilla sablé pastry. Using a wooden spoon or your hands, blend the ingredients until they come together.

Sift in the flour, plus the cocoa powder if you are making chocolate sablé pastry, and work everything together into a firm dough. Shape into a flat slab, wrap in cling film and chill for 1 hour before use (or freeze for later use).

Puff Pastry

Chilled or frozen puff pastry is available in most supermarkets. For the real thing, however, nothing beats home-made. Making puff pastry pleases the technical baker and those with a bit of patience. It seems to us to border on a natural wonder that multiple ultra-thin layers of butter and dough can create such deliciousness.

I have to admit that physics was not my strong point at school, but with puff pastry we have an excellent display of physics in action. Maybe it would be a good way to engage young children in the world of science. The water in the butter evaporates and lifts up a total of 144 very thin layers of dough; meanwhile the gluten in the flour sets and prevents it collapsing – by now I think we are in chemistry territory.

The quantities below make enough for three 20cm tarts. You can divide the pastry in three and store two pieces in the freezer.

500g strong white flour
1 tbsp caster sugar
1 tsp salt
500g unsalted butter
200ml cold water

Place 425g of the flour in a large mixing bowl with the sugar and salt. Dice 50g of the butter and rub it into the flour with your fingertips. Add the water and stir to make a fairly stiff dough, being careful not to over-mix. Shape into a square slab, wrap in cling film and leave in the fridge for about 45 minutes. Meanwhile, cut the rest of the butter into large cubes, sprinkle with the remaining 75g flour, then knead the flour into the butter. Shape it into a flat slab, roughly the surface area of 4 standard butter packs. Wrap in cling film and chill for about 30 minutes.

Now it's time to layer the puff pastry. Remove the dough and the butter mixture from the fridge and unwrap them. Altogether, I generally give the pastry 2 'letter' and 2 'book' folds – a letter fold creates 3 layers and a book fold 4. Roll the dough into a square sheet double the size of the butter pad.

Place the butter pad on top of the dough at a 45-degree angle, then seal it like an envelope by folding the dough over it so that it encloses the butter pad completely.

Roll out into a long, oblong sheet about 1cm thick, then fold the top third down towards the middle and the bottom third over the top, like folding a letter. This is your first letter fold. Wrap in cling film and chill for 30 minutes.

Now you need to give the pastry a book fold. Remove from the fridge and roll into a long, oblong sheet about 1cm thick. Fold both short ends in so they meet in the middle, then fold one half over the other, like closing a book. Wrap in cling film and chill for 30 minutes.

Remove from the fridge and repeat the steps for one letter fold and one book fold, then chill for 30 minutes before using.

Butter Shortbread

This is a useful recipe if you are getting to know a new oven or making the first tentative steps on the way to becoming a bake-off champion. It can be rolled out and cut into biscuits or used as a quick and versatile base for all sorts of tray bakes, including Bakewell Slab (see page 139) and the moreish Ninja Slice (page 136).

120g unsalted butter, cut into cubes
120g plain flour
60g semolina
60g caster sugar, plus extra for sprinkling

Put all the ingredients in a freestanding electric mixer and, using the paddle attachment, mix until they form fine, sticky crumbs. Alternatively, put them in a mixing bowl and rub them together by hand.

If you want to use the mixture to make biscuits, bring the crumbs together into a dough and roll out like pastry, then cut out with a biscuit cutter. Bake at 180°C/Gas Mark 4 for about 14 minutes, until a light golden colour. To use as a base for a tray bake, follow the directions in your recipe.

To make petticoat tails, spread the mixture evenly over the base of a lined 22–25cm springform cake tin or loose-bottomed tart tin and flatten with your fingertips or the back of a large spoon. Place in an oven preheated to 180°C/Gas Mark 4 and bake for 20 minutes or until just turning golden brown. Remove from the oven and sprinkle with a little caster sugar, if you wish. Cut into wedges while the shortbread is still slightly warm, then leave in the tin to cool completely.

Streusel (Crumble)

Streusel is a very versatile topping for cakes and tarts but can also be pressed into a tin to form a base instead of sweet pastry or shortbread. You can scatter it over plums, rhubarb, apples and blackberries and bake to make a warming dessert.

In Germany streusel tends to be coarse and lumpy, especially when sprinkled straight on to dough for a homely Streuselkuchen (use the Bun Dough opposite if you'd like to make this). To achieve a coarser texture, it's best to use cold butter and the dough hook on a freestanding electric mixer. For a finer crumble, use softer butter and the paddle attachment, or the whisks on a handheld electric mixer.

I usually make a small quantity by hand rather than with an electric mixer. I choose the butter temperature according to the texture I desire, then rub the ingredients together briefly for a fine texture or for longer to give a coarse, lumpy texture.

170g plain flour
100g caster sugar
100g salted butter, cut into small cubes

Put all the ingredients in a bowl. Mix either with an electric mixer or by hand. If mixing by hand, mix the flour and sugar together, add the cubed butter, then, using quick movements, use your fingertips to rub the mixture together until it forms a clumpy consistency.

Bun Dough

Bun dough can be used in many different ways: as a base for fruit tray bakes, stuffed with jam or fruit, plaited to make a sweet loaf, or for the lovely Beasty Buns on page 157. It is really easy to make, especially after you have done it a few times, and has the advantage of being less fragile than pastry when you handle or roll it. It does require more time but a lot of that is resting time, leaving you to get on with other activities – or have a rest yourself. The quantity given here is quite small, so it can be made by hand. Skip the gym workout and knead your dough for 3–5 minutes instead.

For the yeast to multiply and ferment, you need the right conditions: the correct temperature, plus moisture, nourishment and, perhaps hardest of all, a little time and patience.

300g strong white flour
20g fresh yeast or a 7g sachet of dried yeast
100ml milk, at room temperature
1 tsp honey
50g caster sugar
50g unsalted butter, softened
1 medium egg
a small pinch of salt

To help the dough ferment, I like to make a small starter to give the yeast the chance to multiply and provide the necessary lift during baking. The ideal temperature for the yeast to develop in the starter is 25–28°C. If the other ingredients are very cold, you can warm the milk to about 30–35°C, but no more or it will kill the yeast.

To make the starter, sift half the flour into a bowl and crumble the fresh yeast over the top, or stir in the dried yeast. Add the milk and honey and mix together with a spatula – towards the end it might be easier to use your hands to shape the dough into a smooth ball.

Cover with cling film and leave for 1–2 hours at room temperature, until it doubles in size. For a speedier process, find a warm place for it to rest in. If you don't have a plate-warming cabinet or airing cupboard, the top of electrical equipment is often surprisingly warm.

Add the rest of the flour, plus all the remaining ingredients, and bring together into a rough dough. Knead it either with an electric mixer fitted with a dough hook or by hand. It might be quite sticky at first but, as you knead, it will become smoother and silkier. If you do it by hand, transfer the dough to a work surface and stretch and turn it intensively for 3–5 minutes. It's a little workout and does wonders for your hands – enjoy it.

Return the dough to the bowl and cover with cling film. Leave until doubled in size again, then use as directed in your recipe.

Almond Cream

(Frangipane)

Almond cream is one of those basic recipes that are well worth remembering. It is simply equal parts of butter, sugar, eggs and almonds plus 10 per cent plain flour. Use plain in summery berry tarts (see page 111) or add even greater depths of flavour with a little orange zest, rosewater or orange flower water.

100g salted butter, softened
100g caster sugar
2 medium eggs, lightly beaten
100g ground almonds
10g plain flour

Beat the butter and sugar together until light and fluffy. Gradually add the beaten eggs, alternating with the ground almonds.

Finally mix in the flour. The almond cream will keep in the fridge for 5 days.

Light Meringue

The basic recipe for standard meringues is 1 part egg white to 2 parts sugar. As a topping on baked fruit tarts, however, I prefer a lighter meringue, consisting of 1 part egg white to 1½ parts sugar.

5 egg whites (about 150ml)
a pinch of salt
225g caster sugar

Always whisk egg whites in an ultra-clean mixing bowl without any hint of grease or fat. Wash the bowl in hot soapy water, then rinse with cold water. If possible, add a squeeze of lemon juice before drying it with kitchen paper.

Now add the egg whites and salt. Using a hand whisk or a freestanding electric mixer fitted with the whisk attachment, start whipping the egg whites at low speed.

When they begin to get frothy, add a couple of tablespoons of the sugar and increase the speed to high. Gradually beat in all the remaining sugar until you have a soft-peaked meringue. Use immediately.

Lavender Sugar

Lavender sugar is now available in supermarkets but it is just as easy to mix your own. Use it to flavour the Orange and Lavender Crunch Cake on page 47 or the Lavender Shortbread on page 95.

You can also make lavender scones: follow the recipe on page 162 but omit the sultanas and replace the sugar with lavender sugar.

Simply put 500g golden caster sugar in a jar and add 4 tablespoons of dried culinary lavender or any lavender that has not been treated with pesticides – perhaps your own home-grown. Seal in an airtight jar and leave for at least a week to infuse. Sift out the coarser bits of lavender before use.

Vanilla Sugar

Vanilla sugar is one of those magic ingredients that can add some wow factor to your recipes, yet in our fast-paced world we think we don't have the time it takes to leave the two to infuse – ideally for at least a week.

It can be used in sponge cakes and biscuits, or enjoyed sprinkled over freshly baked shortbread or even added to a fruit salad for a touch of sweetness.

If you start from scratch and want 'instant' vanilla sugar, use 1 vanilla pod to about 250g caster sugar. It's more economical, however, to mix scraped-out vanilla pods with sugar and infuse it for a longer period in a tightly sealed jar. At Konditor & Cook we have a big bucket of sugar into which we put all the empty vanilla pods. There is plenty of residual flavour left in them and this is the best way to extract it.

Cream Cheese Frosting

This basic frosting recipe can easily be adapted. The thickness of the frosting depends on the consistency of the cream cheese you use. You may have to add more icing sugar if it is too wet.

At Konditor & Cook we use the cream cheese supplied to us by our dairy, which is relatively firm, with a creamy colour. However, for this book all the recipes have been tested using the widely available full-fat Philadelphia cheese. It makes a lighter frosting but the consistency is very satisfactory.

200g full-fat cream cheese
400g icing sugar
50g unsalted butter

Vanilla: seeds of ½ vanilla pod or
　½ tsp vanilla extract

Raspberry or blackcurrant: 50g frozen raspberry or blackcurrant purée, thawed, or 100g fresh or frozen raspberries or blackcurrants

Coffee: 2 tbsp instant coffee, dissolved in
　1 tbsp hot water

Lemon: grated zest of 1 unwaxed lemon

If making raspberry or blackcurrant frosting from whole fruit, heat the fruit until the juices run, then blitz with a handheld blender. Boil until reduced by half, then pass it through a fine sieve to remove the seeds and leave to cool.

Put the cream cheese, icing sugar and any flavouring into a bowl and beat slowly with a handheld electric mixer until smooth. Put the butter in a small pan and soften over a very low heat so that it just disintegrates rather than becoming piping hot. With the hand mixer still on a slow speed, gradually pour the melted butter into the cream cheese mixture until it is completely combined, then whisk it briefly at a higher speed. If you're happy with the consistency use it straight away. If the butter was too warm, the frosting may be a bit soft and will need chilling slightly first.

Royal Icing

Use this for piping decorations or for frosting Christmas cakes and other celebration cakes. You will need 3 times the quantity below to cover a 20cm cake.

1 medium egg white
1 tbsp lemon juice
250g icing sugar
1 tsp glycerine (optional)

Place the egg white and lemon juice in a bowl and sift in half the icing sugar. Mix with a spatula to form a creamy paste.

Gradually mix in the remaining icing sugar with a wooden spoon or a firm spatula until the mixture is smooth and forms soft peaks. Lift out the spoon to test the peaks; if the icing is too soft, add a little more icing sugar; if it is too stiff, add a few drops of lemon juice or water.

If using the icing immediately, cover with cling film or a damp cloth to prevent a crust forming. Otherwise, store in an airtight container in the fridge for up to 2 weeks. You can freeze the icing in small freezer bags too, but after defrosting you will have to mix it briefly with a spoon and add a little more icing sugar to achieve the correct consistency.

For writing and other decorative elements, use plain or add a little food colouring to create colourful designs. For frosting traditional fruit cakes, add the glycerine to keep the icing slightly softer.

Quick Buttercream

At catering college, I learned three methods for making buttercream, all of them very time consuming and involving endless bowls and whisks. They really aren't practical for home use, when you need only a small amount. Here is a round-up of national preferences:

French buttercream involves slowly beating sugar and eggs together over heat, then continuing to beat until they firm up and become cold, and finally folding the mixture into soft, whipped butter. A very fine and tasty buttercream indeed.

Italian buttercream is made by whipping up egg whites with hot sugar syrup, then folding them into butter (keeps well).

German buttercream is simply butter and sugar beaten until fluffy, with custard folded into it (a childhood favourite of mine).

A quicker method than any of the above is the one in which one part butter is beaten with two parts icing sugar. I find this too sugary, preferring to add some cream cheese to make it taste less sweet. This type of buttercream can be made with minimal fuss and tastes delicious.

150g unsalted butter, softened
75g full-fat cream cheese
300g icing sugar, sifted

Vanilla:
seeds of ½ vanilla pod or ½ tsp vanilla extract

White chocolate:
100g white chocolate, melted

Hazelnut:
see Wheat-free Hazelnut Cupcakes (page 150)

Put the butter and cream cheese, and vanilla if using, into a bowl and whisk with an electric mixer until fluffy.

Reduce the speed of the mixer and add the icing sugar a tablespoon at a time until well combined. If using white chocolate, stir it in now. Increase the speed to high.

Truffle Ganache

This can be used to fill and frost chocolate cakes – for example, as an alternative frosting for the dark chocolate sponge in the Curly Whirly Cake on page 14. It can also be turned into chocolate truffles or a very indulgent hot chocolate drink.

300g dark chocolate
   (54 per cent cocoa solids)
250ml single cream

Chop the chocolate finely and place in a bowl.

Bring the cream just to boiling point and pour it over the chocolate. Stir until it has completely melted and the ganache looks silken and smooth. Freshly made ganache is too soft to use for icing the sides of a cake, so leave it until it starts to thicken but is still shiny. If you run a spoon through and it leaves a furrow that holds its shape, it's ready to use. Once the ganache has set, you can always gently heat it again over a pan of lightly simmering water or in a microwave.

To make truffles, simply leave the ganache to set, then roll spoonfuls of it into balls and drop them into dark cocoa powder or icing sugar to finish (this method is used for making the spider's bodies on page 169). To make hot chocolate, stir 2 heaped tablespoons of the ganache into 200ml hot milk.

Chocolate Icing

This is an easy and low-cost alternative to using a pure chocolate ganache to cover a cake. It is used while still quite runny, so is not suitable for 'crumb coating' a cake – as in the Curly Whirly Cake (page 14), for example. It makes an interesting alternative to the topping for the Orange and Lavender Crunch Cake on page 47.

If you cannot get coconut butter, you can substitute sunflower oil, though it will give a slightly softer result.

150g icing sugar
3 tbsp cocoa powder
25g coconut butter (natural, not coconut-flavoured)

Sift the icing sugar and cocoa powder into a bowl and add 2 tablespoons of hot water. Mix to a smooth paste, using a spatula.

Melt the coconut butter in a saucepan or microwave and mix it into the icing. If it is too stiff to spread on a cake, add a little more hot water. Use immediately.

Mascarpone Frosting

I have fallen in love with this wonderfully creamy, custardy-tasting topping or cake filling. It's so easy to make, has a great texture and can be used in the same ways as the Cream Cheese Frosting on page 211. The cream cheese version contains more sugar; this one is heavier on fat. There's no cake without a bit of sinning, I'm afraid.

75g unsalted butter, softened
75g icing sugar
150g mascarpone cheese

Vanilla:
seeds of ½ vanilla pod or ½ tsp vanilla extract

Coffee:
2 tbsp instant coffee, dissolved in 1 tbsp
   hot water

Noisette:
75g fine noisette dark chocolate, melted

Put the butter in a bowl, sift in the icing sugar and beat until light and fluffy.

Beat in the mascarpone cheese a tablespoon at a time. Add any flavourings and mix well.

Lemon Curd

It's so easy to remember the quantities for this recipe because it uses equal parts of all four ingredients. Lemon curd can be used in lemon meringue pies or folded into whipped cream and used to fill meringues.

100g caster sugar
100g unsalted butter, diced
juice of 2 lemons (about 100ml)
2 medium eggs

Place all the ingredients in a heatproof bowl and set it over a pan of simmering water, making sure the water doesn't touch the base of the bowl.

Cook, stirring constantly, until the mixture starts to thicken. To check whether it's thick enough, dip a wooden spoon into the curd, then run your finger down the back of it; it should leave a clear channel.

Pour the curd into a clean bowl and leave to cool. You can dust a little icing sugar on top, if you like, to prevent a skin forming. The curd will keep in a very clean sealed container in the fridge for 2 weeks.

Orange Curd
Replace the lemon juice with orange juice.

Custard

This basic custard is great served alongside Apple Strudel (see page 75).

300ml milk
2 tbsp caster sugar
½ vanilla pod, slit open lengthways
2 tbsp cornflour
1 medium egg yolk

Put 250ml of the milk in a small pan with the sugar and vanilla pod and bring to boiling point.

Put the cornflour into a small bowl, add the remaining milk and the egg yolk and blend with a fork.

When the milk is boiling, remove it from the heat and whisk the egg yolk mixture into it until it thickens. If necessary, put it back on the heat for a few moments and stir until thickened. You don't need to let it boil again; just seeing the small bubbles moving from the outside of the pan towards the centre will suffice.

Tips and Techniques

How to butter and flour a cake tin

Buttering and flouring a cake tin is preferable when you want the cake to retain the shape of the tin rather than shrink away from the edges and contract slightly, as it will do with baking parchment. This is also the only method to use for intricate bundt cake tins.

Gently melt some butter (or coconut butter or oil if you are making a dairy-free cake). Using a pastry brush, grease the inside of the tin with an even coating of the butter. Then add enough plain flour to the tin to cover the inside in a thin layer.

Turn the tin upside down and shake out the excess flour on to a large piece of baking parchment (this way you can gather it up and reuse it).

How to line a cake tin with baking parchment

Springform tin (base only)

Release the base of the springform tin from the ring, then grease the inside of the ring with butter. Tear off a piece of baking parchment slightly larger than the base. Place it on the base, then put the ring on top and clamp it on. If you wish, use scissors to cut away the excess parchment, leaving 1cm all round.

Springform tin (base and sides) or for lining a pastry case for blind baking

Place the tin on a sheet of baking parchment, making sure there is an extra 5cm paper all round it. Mark the circumference of the tin on the paper with the back of a knife. Remove the tin, then, using scissors, cut out the circle with an extra 5cm-wide ring all round it (i.e. an extra 10cm diameter). Cut this 5cm ring into a fringe by snipping 1cm-wide strips from the edge to the inner ring.

Centre the paper base in the springform tin; the strips will bend upwards, slightly overlap and thus cover the sides.

This method can also be used to line pastry cases for blind baking. In this case, you need to check the inner diameter of the tart and cut out a piece of baking parchment to fit, adding the height of the tart to form a big enough ring.

How to line a cake tin with foil

Foil is more suitable than baking parchment for very liquid cake mixes and for upside-down cakes. Tear off a piece of foil large enough to cover the base and sides of your tin, then gently press it down in the middle of the base.

Smooth it carefully towards the side of the tin, using the back of your index fingers to push the foil into the edges.

Sloping-sided moule à manqué tins are easily lined by pushing the foil into the tin with a second tin.

How to make rustic paper cases for muffins

Commercial muffins are often baked in brown or black tulip paper cases. Baking parchment does not bend easily, but there is a trick you can use to make your own home-made version.

Cut some baking parchment into 15cm squares. Immerse them briefly in water, then remove and shake off the excess. Centre each square over an indent of the muffin tin and, using your index and middle fingers, press them down into the tin. They will then take on the shape of the indent, with the corners pointing upwards.

Ovens and temperatures

If you are baking in a new oven, I strongly advise buying an oven thermometer to check that the display correlates with the actual temperature. I have found that ovens can be out by up to 30°C, leading to the cake either undercooking or burning before the centre is cooked.

Generally I prefer to bake cakes in the middle of the oven with basic top or bottom heat rather than fan assisted. My own oven has four runners and I bake on the second one up. If you use a fan-assisted oven, you will need to reduce the cooking temperatures in this book by 20°C.

Fan ovens are good for meringues or when baking multiple trays of biscuits or cookies.

How to make a parchment piping bag

Cut a 30cm x 15cm x 25cm triangle from a piece of baking parchment. Lay it flat on a work surface with the longest side on your left (or the other way round if you are left handed). Curl the top corner towards you and to the right (or the left, if you are left handed), forming a cone.

Hold it together with your thumb and index finger. While still holding it, curl the bottom corner up and around the cone. Now pick up the tip of the cone with your other hand and remove your thumb and index finger from the opening of the cone. Tuck what used to be the bottom corner inside the opening of the cone to stop it unfolding.

A few tips on piping

Make a parchment piping bag as described above and fill it with a walnut-sized dollop of icing, melted chocolate or ganache. Place the bag on a flat surface with the seam at the bottom.

Roll up the open end like a tube of toothpaste, thus sealing the opening and tightening the seam. Use scissors to cut the desired opening in the tip – 2–3mm for writing, for example.

Rather than looking at the piping bag as a substitute for a pen and holding and using it that way, think of piping as more like an application, where you are laying down a thread of icing.

Start with the piping bag held close to the surface and squeeze gently so the icing starts to come out. Then, still squeezing gently to create an unbroken thread of icing, raise the tip of the bag so it is 1–2cm above the surface and keep it at this level as you pipe.

Press the icing out of the bag with your right thumb (or your left if you are left handed) and keep the seam tensioned.

Guide the tip of the piping bag with the index and middle finger of your other hand – this makes the writing less shaky.

What chocolate should I use?

For baking and where we add sugar to the recipe anyway, at Konditor & Cook we tend to use dark chocolate with 54 per cent cocoa solids, such as Callebaut chocolate chips (known as callets), which are available online.

In some cases, such as in brownies, we specify chocolate with 70 per cent cocoa solids, as the chocolate is added in chip form and hardly melts, releasing its flavour when you eat it. Be aware that 70 per cent chocolate burns easily (especially in a microwave) and can develop a bitter taste if overcooked.

How to temper chocolate

If you are not using chocolate buttons (or chips), chop three-quarters of the chocolate into rough pieces and place them in a bowl set over a pan filled with cold water.

Start heating the water, stirring the chocolate occasionally as it begins to melt. Once the water starts to simmer, remove the bowl, as it should not get too hot.

While the chocolate is melting, chop the remaining chocolate into fine pieces. Very small chocolate buttons can be used whole but ones of 1.5cm or more need to be chopped.

Decant roughly a third of the melted chocolate into a bowl. Try to keep it warm (over the pan of hot water with the heat turned off, for example).

Add the finely chopped chocolate to the remaining two-thirds of the melted chocolate to bring the temperature down to approximately 27°C for dark chocolate or 25°C for white chocolate, stirring with a spatula until all the pieces are more or less melted. You could also leave the chocolate to cool down at room temperature (a slow method), or place it in the fridge (a quicker method, but it will need regular stirring).

Now add the warm melted chocolate back to the bowl; this should raise the temperature by a few degrees, ideally to 31–32°C for dark chocolate, 28–29°C for white chocolate.

At this point, take a sample to see if it is correctly tempered. Dip a knife or spatula into the chocolate, shake off the excess and leave to set at room temperature. After a minute you should notice a soft sheen at the edges as it starts to set. Great news! If it stays glossy and does not set, it is too warm. In this case, add more chocolate to cool it down to 27°C or 25°C again, then bring it back up to 31–32°C (dark chocolate) or 28–29°C (white chocolate) by warming it for a few seconds over the pan of hot water. If you don't have more chocolate to add, you can cool it down in the fridge for a few minutes, then warm it back up.

It is helpful to have a thermometer for all this, but without one you can make some checks using Mother Nature. Body temperature is around 36–37°C; if you dip the side of your little finger in the chocolate and it feels warm, the temperature is higher than your body temperature, if it feels cool, you are on the right track. Remember, though, that it needs to have formed an emulsion – which means going from warm to cool to correctly tempered.

Index

Acknowledgements

Konditor & Cook is a London-based, twenty-first-century family business, employing people from all over the world, so I'd like to start by thanking all the hundreds of talented individuals who have helped cement our reputation over the last 20 years.

Of course I wouldn't even be a baker or be in London if it wasn't for my family and friends back in Germany. Vielen Dank!

As regards the book, big thanks go to my agent, Juliet Pickering, and the Ebury team: Sarah Lavelle and Laura Higginson. It all seemed to go very smoothly!

I'm in awe of editor Jane Middleton – her patience and ability to ask all the right questions have hopefully made the recipes in this book easy enough to follow. A special thank you to her 12-year-old daughter for testing some of the recipes along the way, proving they are child's play.

Thanks to Cynthia Inions' wizardry, sourcing crockery and backgrounds, and, of course, Jean Cazals' magical photography and Jamie Wieck's fantastic design and patterns throughout. This book has turned out to be a feast for the eyes.

Finally I would like to thank my partner Paul Cons for running the company and for encouraging me to write this book. I love him nearly as much as I love cake.

10 9 8 7 6 5 4 3 2 1

Published in 2014 by Ebury Press, an imprint of Ebury Publishing
A Random House Group Company

The Random House Group Limited Reg. No. 954009

Addresses for companies within the Random House Group can be found at www.randomhouse.co.uk
A CIP catalogue record for this book is available from the British Library.

The Random House Group Limited supports the Forest Stewardship Council® (FSC®), the leading
international forest-certification organisation. Our books carrying the FSC label are printed on FSC®-
certified paper. FSC is the only forest-certification scheme supported by the leading environmental
organisations, including Greenpeace. Our paper procurement policy can be found at www.random-
house.co.uk/environment

To buy books by your favourite authors and register for offers visit www.randomhouse.co.uk

Copy editor: Jane Middleton
Art Direction: ENSO
Design: Pete & Jim
Photography: Jean Cazals
Stylist: Cynthia Inions

Colour origination by Altaimage, London
Printed and bound in Germany by Mohn Media GmbH

ISBN 9780091957599